LOS ANGELES REVIEW OF BOOKS QUARTERLY JOURNAL | WINTER 2016

COVER ART
MILJOHN RUPERTO AND RINI YUN KEAGY
COURTESY OF THE ARTISTS AND KOENIG & CLINTON

The Los Angeles Review of Books is a 501(c)(3) nonprofit organization. The *LARB Quarterly Journal* is published quarterly by the Los Angeles Review of Books, 6671 Sunset Blvd., Suite 1521, Los Angeles, CA 90028. Submissions for the *Journal* can be emailed to EDITORIAL@LAREVIEWOFBOOKS.ORG. Visit our website at WWW.LAREVIEWOFBOOKS.ORG.

The *LARB Quarterly Journal* is a premium of the LARB Membership Program. Annual subscriptions are available. Go to WWW.LAREVIEWOFBOOKS.ORG/MEMBERSHIP for more information or email MEMBERSHIP@LAREVIEWOFBOOKS.ORG.

Distribution through Publishers Group West. If you are a retailer and would like to order the *LARB Quarterly Journal*, call 800-788-3123 or email orderentry@perseusbooks.com.

PIETER SCHOOLWERTH
AFTER TROY 7, 2012
OIL, ACRYLIC, GICLÉE PRINT AND OIL PASTEL ON CANVAS; 73 X 54"
COURTESY THE ARTIST AND MIGUEL ABREU GALLERY, NEW YORK; PHOTO: JEFFREY STURGES

DAK
Fully Cooked • Water Added
Premium Ham
Nutrition Facts
Serving Size: 2 oz (56g)
Servings Per Container: 8
Amount Per Serving
Calories 100 Calories from Fat 60
% Daily Values*
Total Fat 7g 10%
Saturated Fat 2g 11%
Trans Fat 0g
Cholesterol 40mg 13%
Sodium 620mg 26%
Total Carbohydrate 0%
Less than 1g
Sugars less than 1g
Protein 9g

CON TENTS

< ANISSA MACK
CATHEDRAL (OAK), 2013
HAM CAN, AMETHYST CRYSTALS;
8 1/2 X 7 X 7"
COURTESY OF THE ARTIST AND LAUREL GITLEN, NEW YORK

J.C. AND O.J.

KANNAN MAHADEVAN

I DOUBT ANYONE remembers J.C. At the height of his fame he appeared on the radio, on a morning show called "Settin' It Straight." He was supposed to do an interview for *The Diamondback*, and I went around telling everybody that he came inside my house once. Then the world heard about O.J., and forgot J.C.

But we knew him before he got famous. He was always catching us by surprise. On some hazy day at the height of summer, when the world seemed nothing but a stretch of baked concrete sprouting yellow grass, when I couldn't imagine anything looking otherwise or anything at all out of the ordinary, he would appear at the top of the stone steps, with Tyson, his huge black and brown Rottweiler, barking and panting in front of the metal gate.

Where he was coming from, where he would ship off to next, J.C. wasn't allowed to say. All we knew was that he was in some special unit, high up in the army, and that his mission was very important. Black George never complained about Dover and the Reserves when J.C. was around. "I'm just a weekend warrior," he said. "He in it for real."

I always wanted to ask J.C. if he had ever killed anyone. But he would say, "I'm home now," looking so serious that we never dared press him. We tried to tell him everything he had missed.

Archie told him about the Howard Johnson murders. A string of people were turning up stabbed in their hotel rooms. The sheets were torn up; the fan was always left on. The killer was said to be marauding the Beltway area. We were told to go straight home from school; all afterschool activities were canceled.

"What's the count?" J.C. asked.

"Four slayings so far," Archie said. This was the word the papers used. Then he added quickly, "He not through yet though."

J.C. didn't seem too impressed. He said he had heard about it. Then he pulled on Tyson's collar and said, "Tyson heard too, didn't you Tyse?"

Tyson went on panting, hanging his tongue out in the heat.

J.C. laughed. "He heard."

J.C. had a way of making our big news seem very small. He had no respect for the media, or celebrities. He said, "Trust me, where the real deal be going down, ain't no cameras."

At the same time he would make a big deal about things we hardly noticed. Once he came home and found that the old green bridge across the creek had been replaced by a new wooden one. He went around asking everybody, "When they do this?" Nobody could tell him; a few people noticed it for the first time. J.C. laughed and said there must have been some construction. Black George agreed.

"How you going live in a place, have something change right in front of you, and not know when it happened?"

I thought and thought, wanting to be the one who could tell him. I could remember the old green bridge, the way the metal rang when you clambered over it. I saw the new bridge, wooden and clearly newly built. But I had no idea when one became the other.

"And this is your home," J.C. sighed.

When he was home, J.C. spent half his time staying with whichever woman he was seeing. We never saw these women when J.C. was abroad. But they always seemed to come out when he was back, and sometimes he rotated between the houses of two or three. Gina was the one he stuck with most. She was big, older-looking than J.C., with dark green tattoos on her chest. She worked at a Jasper's somewhere and sometimes she brought leftovers to the courts in Styrofoam containers.

At one point J.C. said they were spending all their time together — cooking, watching movies, or just lying around, reading the paper, wasting the day together. He made it all sound very peaceful. He said, "Now that's the kind of woman I need. Someone I can make a home with. Gina, she into board games. She got me playing Scrabble!"

"Scrabble!" Black George said. "That's worse than golf."

J.C. shrugged. "We just going be boring together, I guess." And when he smiled he looked like somebody in a commercial, with his straight white teeth and his hair gleaming and greased back against his head; and I had no trouble imagining him doing dependable things like mowing lawns and waxing cars, and all the jobs around the house my mother called her "shit work."

For a little while we all saw J.C. being very domestic. I saw him and Gina as I walked to the bus stop. They were jogging along the creek in matching gray sweat suits, with Tyson trotting at their side. When the dog pulled on his leash, J.C. said in a loud, practiced voice, "Ay! Ay, Tyse!" And they stopped when they saw me, jogging in place as they talked. That was in the morning.

After school let out, in the late afternoon, he rolled into the parking lot in his dusty old pickup truck. Tyson stuck his huge head out the open window and barked, and J.C. let him roam around, splashing him with water before chaining him up against the fence. Around evening Gina came, off work, and sat on the bench and clapped as he played.

"Coach," he was saying to me, "this backhand of mine is keeping me back. Show me how you hit yours." J.C. said my backhand was smooth, like water; and I always liked showing it to him because it was something I had never really worked on and something he would never really get. But now Gina came onto the court in her high heels, asking how to hit the ball, and J.C. held her shoulders and moved her arms, and everybody stood by and watched and gave advice, as though he were parking a car.

It all lasted for about two weeks. One day J.C. came to the courts alone. Black George asked, "Where Gina at?"

J.C. said, "Wherever she at."

We knew it was over.

And a few days later J.C. and Black George and Archie were talking about their annual trip to the Stardust Inn, home of the two topless dancers Go-Go and Nightshade.

In between women, J.C. stayed at his mother's house in Bladensburg, a few miles outside of DC. She had lived alone for years; for her birthday one year J.C. had surprised her with Tyson, as a guard dog; and now he was her only companion when J.C. was gone. When he talked about his mother I thought he sounded like he was being interviewed.

"She was the one who taught me to work," he said. "She used to say to me, 'Your hands can do anything. It's only your eyes that get afraid.' One job wasn't enough for her. She always had two or three. That's where I got my sense of discipline."

I imagined J.C. climbing a cement stoop on a block of row houses, knocking on a plain red door. An old woman would take a long time to appear in the doorway, and cry when she saw who it was.

But then one day J.C. brought his mother to the courts, as a special outing, and we were all shocked. J.C. said she was only in her late 60s. She was almost bald, with only a few strands of silver hair left. My back hurt when I saw how bent over she was, and I couldn't help shivering when her metal walker scraped against the cement. She didn't seem like she could do any work. It was all behind her. J.C., looking like a DC statue in his army uniform, kept saying, "She raised me up."

Everybody stopped playing and greeted her with respect. She grabbed my wrist and said, "Jerome takes care of me!" I didn't know what to say. Her gold bangle was pressing against my wrist bone. J.C. smiled proudly. Then, still holding my wrist, she turned to J.C. and said, "When are you going to settle down, boy?"

We laughed politely, to show we didn't take her seriously. But then we saw tears in her eyes, and she whined in a desperate way, "When are you going to stop fooling around and settle *down*?"

She stamped her foot and squeezed my hand, and suddenly I couldn't look at her anymore. Even her frustration seemed so useless and worn-out. J.C. said quietly, "Soon." And he took her hand off mine and led her down the hill to the parking lot.

Later he explained, "She has good days and bad."

Before he shipped back out, J.C. asked Black George and Archie to look in on his mother if they got a chance.

"But don't tell her I sent you," he said. "Tell her you were in the neighborhood. She getting on, but she don't want nobody thinking she can't take care of herself. She too proud."

Black George was flattered. He said, "This is how it should be."

"I'ma visit with her this weekend," Archie said.

But Black George said he would be in Dover that weekend. The next weekend, Archie was busy, and neither wanted the other to go without him. For about a month they planned to "visit with her." Black George suggested bringing her some flowers for Mother's Day and saying they were from J.C.

"What we going say?" Archie said. "'Here go some roses. Your son sent them. They from the Middle East.' She old, but she not old enough to believe that."

"How you know that's where he at?" Black George asked.

I brought up the time J.C. had said summer in DC was nothing compared to where he had just come from, and that seemed to settle it: he was in the desert somewhere.

By the time May and Mother's Day came, J.C. had been gone a few months, and we had forgotten him. There was nothing to remind us. Not Tyson, not Gina. I even forgot my own mother, and she would have forgotten too, if some charity hadn't sent her a card showing a big stupid painting of a woman bathing her baby in a bucket.

"Treat me like filth, dirt," my mother said, sorting the mail and muttering as though I weren't there. "Not one iota of appreciation."

The card was left out on a shelf for me to see; then after a week or so she crossed out the Mother's Day greeting and sent it to her sister as a birthday card.

Summer came. Again the world was a baked, empty place. And, finally, because he actually was in the neighborhood — to try out a ribs place on Bladensburg Road — Archie looked in on J.C.'s mother and found that she was dead. A neighbor had found her months ago, in the middle of the floor. Tyson had been barking day and night.

I had never known a person who died. I tried to feel as sad as I could, but all I really felt was that J.C.'s mother was like the old green bridge. First there, then gone.

I told my mother.

"Poor woman," she said. "All alone." Her voice was soft and sweet, and I watched her closely. Her eyes seemed to become wet by magic.

"They found her on the floor."

"Oh *Bhagwan*," my mother wailed.

"Face-down on the floor."

"Why tell me all this?" she snapped, looking up at me accusingly. "You like to see me cry?" I shook my head quickly, afraid that the moment was lost. I didn't know how to tell her I did like to see her cry, but not in the way she meant. She gave a long snort and went back to what she was doing.

Sometimes I wondered where and when the news reached J.C. Maybe he read the letter in a bunk bed while everybody else was sleeping. Or in a big hall surrounded by eating soldiers and clattering plates, or on the sand under the sky. Wherever it was, we saw that he was a changed man. His head was shaved and he wore a black beard up to the hollows under his eyes, and for the first time I thought he looked just like a grim soldier. He set his jaw so that he seemed very determined. But he still sounded like he was being interviewed. He said, "I just need to keep my head up. That's what she always told me."

From now on we knew "she" meant his mother.

"She was right," he said later. "I need to stop fooling around. That was the last thing she told me."

I heard nothing about his women, or the Stardust Inn.

He went to get Tyson out of the pound, where the neighbor had put him. And the dog too was like a different animal. He was skin and bones, and there was no need now to chain him up.

They roamed the neighborhood. J.C., seeming sad and full of thoughts, let his beard grow thick. He began to look lean and grimy from walking all the time. Tyson grew mangy. My mother reported that she had seen them at the Siva Vishnu temple in Greenbelt. J.C. was going around asking people to teach him to meditate, but they wouldn't let the dog inside, so he kicked a shrine and left. I expected my mother to be scornful. Instead she said, "Poor man," and without warning took pity on him. One weekend afternoon she saw him walking and told him to come inside for tea. The dog was to stay out.

Gravely, J.C. said hello to me; after that I was ignored. It was strange to have this man in the house. I could smell his sweat, and once he got up to get some water and banged his head on the chandelier. Other than that, he stayed seated, kept his legs carefully crossed, and listened to my mother talk about God.

She asked his birth date and told him his gemstone was cat's eye. She told him Friday was his auspicious day of the week. She wrote all this out with a fountain pen on a square of paper, and blew on the ink. After J.C. had folded it up and put it in his wallet, she said in an unexpectedly delicate way, "He tells me your mother is no more." I looked up and found that I was being pointed at.

"Yes."

"That is hard. You were close?"

J.C. bowed his head.

"This one" — my mother was pointing at me again — "forgot me on the Day of the Mother. Like I don't exist."

"Mother's Day," I groaned.

J.C. smiled without looking at me. "I always got her roses on Mother's Day. I had them delivered to her door."

My mother began to sniffle, because she got no roses.

"Pray for her," she said, crying for herself, and led him to the door.

After this I felt shy around J.C. I thought he would remember me as the boy who bought no roses. But he didn't seem to remember anything specific. He told me that my mother was a wise woman, and he did begin to pray. Not at the temple, but at the A.M.E. church on Good Luck Road. I lost no time in telling my mother.

"Let him," she said, pretending not to be snubbed. "Like I care where the man goes to pray. Church, bus, hotel, motel."

Meanwhile, J.C. said he hadn't felt so at peace in a long time. "She took me every Sunday when I was little," he said. "And when I stopped, she told me, 'When you need Him again, He'll be there.'"

Shortly after he found religion, J.C. began to jog again. He shaved his beard and wore a necklace with a gold cross on it and put a silver stud in his ear. One day he jogged by the courts and announced that he was getting married. He couldn't stay long; all the time he talked he was jogging in place and smiling and panting.

"When?" Black George demanded.

"Soon."

"You been keeping somebody from us?"

"I'm asking Gina."

"Oh."

I was disappointed that I would have to see her again. For a while nobody could think of anything to say. J.C. was bobbing up and down.

"She still working at Jasper's?"

J.C. shrugged. "I haven't seen her yet. But my mother was right. And Gina, she the kind of woman I could settle down with. I was trifling last time, but now I know."

For the next few weeks we got regular updates. At first Gina refused to see him, saying he had broken her heart. J.C. decided to wait a bit to ask her to marry him.

"She got a point," he said calmly. "I can't just walk into her life and start demanding things. We not two teenagers going buck wild. We adults. You got to give these things time."

They began to talk on the phone. They talked about big things like God and death, and their mothers, and children. J.C. said he told her things he had never told another human soul.

"About the army?" I asked.

J.C. nodded.

We were silent, with awe; and I no longer wondered if J.C. had killed anybody.

He made it a point to confess something new in every phone call. When they were man and wife, he said, there could be no secrets. I begged and begged to hear more, and finally he told us about a time he was on leave.

"I was coming out of a restaurant one night," he said. "I saw my buddy coming toward me down the road. He was riding an elephant covered in purple silk. I could barely see him because he had women all up on him. It was more of them running alongside him and behind the elephant. When he saw me he shouted 'Don't look now, boy!' and grabbed me up with him." A faraway look came into J.C.'s eyes, and he began to rub his head. "All the women *in* the joint emptying out on us, we riding through the streets like kings ..." He trailed off.

We stared at him in amazement. Black George said, "You told Gina that?"

Suddenly J.C. became very solemn. "No secrets," he said.

Then for a couple weeks we didn't see J.C. This seemed like an eternity, we were so addicted to his confessions.

Black George and Archie formed a deputation. They went to the room he was staying in in College Park and knocked on his door; and they came back with an even more sensational story.

"He hiding out!" Black George told me.

What happened was this. One night J.C. called Gina over and over, but she didn't answer. He got so worried that he called 911 and told them his fiancée was a creature of habit and she wasn't answering the phone on her night off. They laughed at this and transferred him to the nonemergency line. So he got in his pickup truck and drove to her house. When he banged on the door, another man came out. Before he could stop himself J.C. had broken the man's nose and two of his teeth.

"Gina prolly too embarrassed to report it," Black George said. "Same with the man, after he got stole."

Eventually J.C. felt so guilty that he reported it himself, in full military regalia at the police station in Hyattsville. The police thought it was a funny story. They also said you couldn't press charges against yourself.

Meanwhile, I was going around telling everyone at school my own version. I made sure to include all the inside details, to prove that I knew J.C. from before. I always started by mentioning his mother, and the time he came inside my house for a spiritual consultation.

When Archie told it, the man who answered the door was naked and smoking a Black & Mild.

Black George called it in to his favorite morning show, the one about domestic disputes he always listened to on the drive to Dover. They wanted to hear it from J.C. himself, who was feeling a little better now that it was clear he was safe. So he went down to the DC studio and got on the air. Travis, the host, introduced him as "Sergeant Jerome Curtis the Third, Emeritus." J.C., for his part, said all the things we had always heard him say.

"Travis," he said, "I don't like to fight. I don't like it. But my mother, she always used to say two things worth fighting for are freedom and family."

"What about your fiancée?" Travis asked. "What did her mama tell *her*?"

"Oh," J.C. chuckled. "That man, he was only somebody from work. She was trying to show him the door."

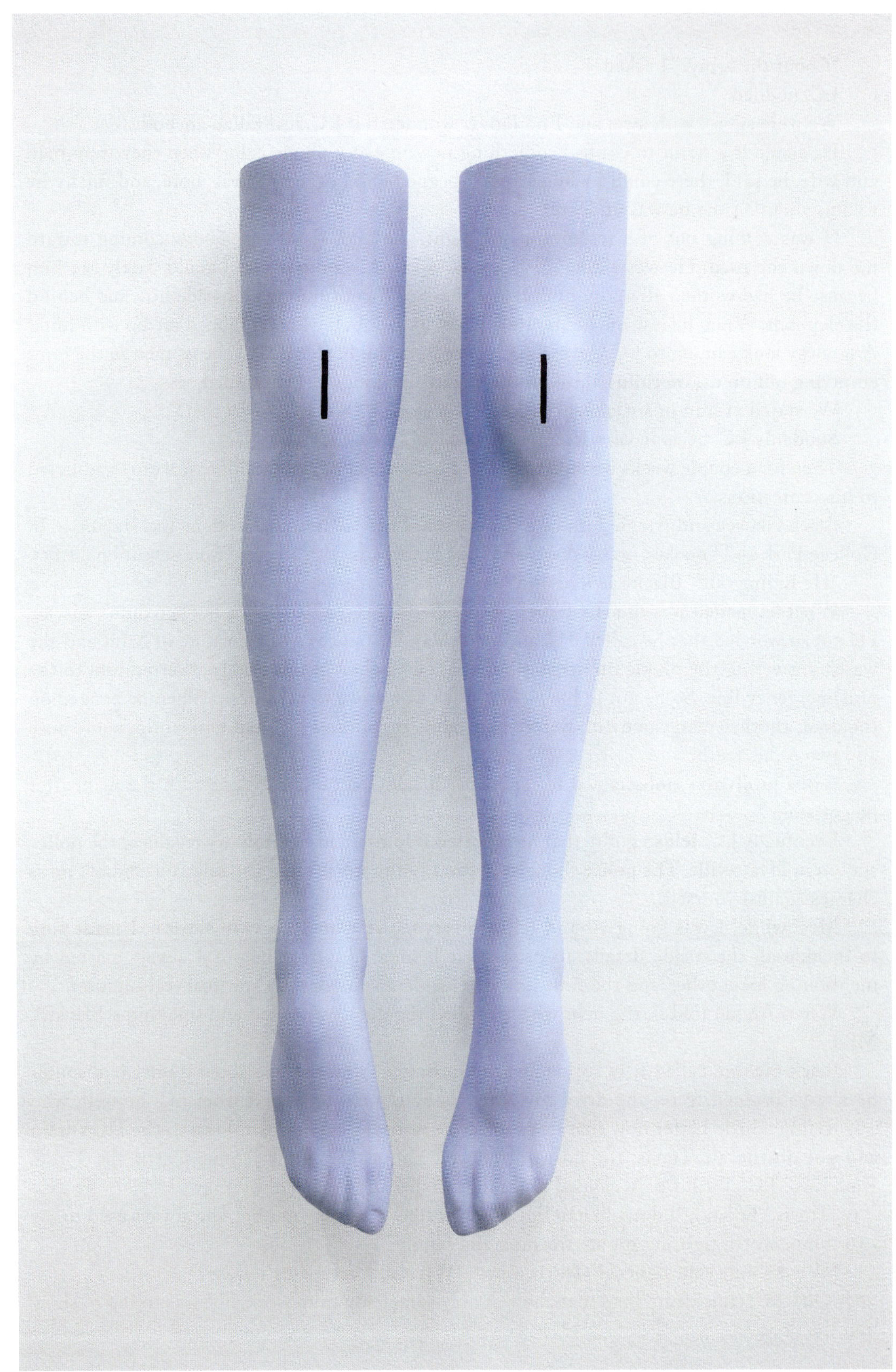

"And you held it open for him?"

"You could say that."

The Diamondback called. Some journalism student from the University of Maryland had heard the show; she wanted to do a profile on J.C. for one of the paper's Community Columns. She sent him a little list of interview questions. He went over his answers carefully with us. He didn't want to sound too arrogant. But he wanted to be thorough. After a month or so he broke down and called Gina. "What can I say?" he said. "I need her help. She knows me better than I know me." Gina assured him that the man he had beaten up was only someone from work she had been trying to get rid of, and told him many things about himself that he had forgotten. In the end the original questions were only a rough guide. I could only get through the first 10 pages of the manuscript — about his childhood in Bladensburg. Archie said there was much more: about his mother who was always in the principal's office, and his teenage years on the streets, before the part about joining up and learning discipline and defending freedom. When it was all finished, J.C. and Gina forgave each other everything, and got jointly baptized in a lake somewhere.

But by that time the whole country had exploded with news of O.J. Simpson, the black football player accused of killing his white ex-wife and her new man. Suddenly there was no place for J.C.'s life story. *The Diamondback*, not to mention the *Post* and the *Times*, reported on nothing but the trial. You couldn't go anywhere in P.G. without seeing men and women wearing huge white T-shirts that said "INNOCENT," with a little J inside the O.

Nobody at the courts wore the shirt. For us, J.C. was the original. O.J. was like a child — he had gone too far. Archie talked about him fondly. "Now who told him to go and do *both* of them? One wasn't enough?"

But I couldn't feel the same way about J.C. after his fame died down. It was hard to be excited anymore when he and Tyson appeared at the top of the stone steps, because Gina was there too. Now that he was finally a family man, he talked to me like I was a little boy. He told me that if I walked with my shoulders back and head up, I would look better and feel better. "I wish I had a father to tell me that when I was your age," he said. When I told him I wished middle school weren't starting so soon, he said, "How you think the world runs? Education. How you think the tanks run? I just operate them, but someone with an education made them that way. Don't let yourself fall behind." But he never again called me Coach and asked to see my backhand.

So I began to avoid him. Soon Gina was pregnant, and they got married and bought a house in the neighborhood. In the driveway behind the old pickup truck appeared a shiny red car like an ugly chariot: the new family minivan. Occasionally you saw J.C. standing at the head of the driveway, surveying his two cars and passing traffic, and nodding at passersby. But more often he was gone, and you saw Gina washing the cars, or mowing the lawn.

< ANISSA MACK
NIGHTSHADE, 2012
PAINTED AQUA RESIN, 25 X 10 X 5"
COURTESY OF THE ARTIST AND LAUREL GITLEN, NEW YORK

WHITNEY HUBBS
UNTITLED, FROM THE ONGOING SERIES, *MY OWN METAPHORS*, 2015
SILVER GELATIN PRINT, 20 X 16"
COURTESY OF THE ARTIST AND M+B GALLERY, LOS ANGELES

Panic KAREN E. BENDER

OCCASIONALLY, MY FOURTH-GRADE teacher at Brentwood Elementary School would shout, "DROP!" This was in the 1970s. She did not say "DROP!" — she yelled it. It sounded like she was going to kill us. But actually she was trying to protect us. When she said this, I always felt like I was going to have a heart attack — a drop drill meant that a nuclear bomb from Russia was about to fall on us. We were supposed to curl under our desks, where we would be safe. There would be a brief thunder of chairs and all of us would dive dramatically under our desks and curl up in balls, hoping the wooden desks would protect us. One unlucky kid would have to be the "blinds monitor," which meant that he or she had to close the blinds so we would not be incinerated by radiation; this person clearly would be the first to die. I don't remember the teacher ever crouching beneath a desk, which would have been an exciting sight, only sitting at her desk, calmly organizing her papers. The drills took about two minutes, but during those minutes, time was very slow.

We waited, foreheads pressed against the linoleum floor, knees tucked to chests, hands clasped over our heads. I remember how close my head came to the other students; I could smell their hair, their shampoo. I thought, generously, that I loved all of them, and then I understood I did not. That girl who had excluded me from four square — well, okay, she could vaporize. That boy, who announced my bad math grade to the class — maybe he could go, too. But their hair seemed so soft — I had an urge to touch the tops of their heads before they vanished. So did I love them? If not, what did I feel? Each one of them was an important part of this thing, my life — perhaps I felt something else.

I remember wondering what aspects of life I would miss if the bomb went off. Would I ever be kissed in a romantic way? Would I ever drive a car? Would I ever go to a restaurant and order a meal by myself? Would someone pay me a lot of money for a skill all my own? Would someone love me? I wondered what part of life I did not want to miss.

The teacher then said, "This is just a drill," which meant that we had to emerge from beneath our desks and return, blinking, to regular life. I remember waiting under the table before I arose, staring at the gray gum roses on the underside of the desk, and, in the moment, feeling strangely safe; I'd beaten something terrible, I thought, even if I had done nothing and there was no bomb. Then I would raise myself to my seat. My hands would, inevitably, be trembling. But for a second, I believed I knew everything.

DOWN DOG BY ANONYMOUS

ELLEN COLLETT

1.

THIS MORNING I KILLED the family dog. Precious had become incontinent, her days spent on a damp doggie bed emitting horrible, keening noises unthinkable in a healthy golden retriever. The vet thought she might have a few good months left, and recommended a canine neurologist who, I found out, would have charged $1,500 for an initial consult and tests. The neurologist's office was an hour away by freeway (two in rush hour), and with no appointment I'd wait, meaning nobody to pick up the kids from school. Weighing the options, I discovered (actually, I'd known for weeks) that a mobile euthanasia service, Down Dog (not their real name), would drive to my house and kill Precious on the spot. I disclose this so you can know the worst of me now. For the record, the pet in question was not a retriever, and what kind of idiot names a dog Precious?

Admitting I killed the family dog will cause problems that even layers of manufactured anonymity might not avert. Two of my oldest friends will certainly drop me without question. "Franny" owns rescues — one three-legged; two of them blind — and volunteers every weekend at an animal shelter in Philly. There, she bathes and walks the most vicious pit bulls and Rottweilers, animals living on the equivalent of Doggie Death Row. (Her name isn't actually Franny, and she lives in a completely different city, maybe not even on the East Coast. She has way more than three dogs, but it's true that most of them are maimed, making Franny a saint for dogs, but sort of a trial where people are concerned.) My other dog-loving friend, "Jen," lives in upstate New York with only two, a Jack Russell terrier and a labradoodle, but sends me regular emails from each of them, like "Dizzy sends kisses!" or "Thelonius hearts you!" Dizzy and Thelonius have their own Facebook pages where they post clever comments beneath photos of themselves napping. Since neither of them can type or use a camera, they've pimped my friend "Jen" — an otherwise brilliant writer — into someone who pens first-person inanities about the joys of licking her privates.

I love dogs, but like Shakespeare wrote, "according to their station / nor more nor less." Meaning, they are not my children, my substitute best friends, or my social crusade. I grew up in rural farm country where dogs were traditionally accorded an independent, outdoor life, less domestic "pets" than free-ranging members of the local fauna. I loved all of them, but never viewed them as members of the family. However, in this day and age, being unsentimental about dogs is not something you admit to publicly without repercussions. The prevailing wisdom says, if you can't love a dog unconditionally there's something really wrong with you.

About Precious: we raised her from babyhood — she and my youngest were born two weeks apart. They were toddlers together. According to dog-year math, Precious entered adolescence while my daughter was just mastering small motor skills, but "Terrible Two" is not so different from "Terrible Teen," and they continued to mirror each other in ways that accentuated their affinities over their differences. Though a dog is not a child. Precious was an exceptionally fine dog. Good-natured, funny, and, toward the end, stoic in her suffering. If she never had a Facebook page, that fault is mine alone.

2.

I recently asked an acquaintance who conducts test screenings for Hollywood movie studios whether there was a single villain "archetype" universally despised by audiences, a character considered completely unredeemable. The answer I expected was the pedophile, the soulless corporate raider, or the ISIL terrorist with a suitcase dirty bomb and a hard-on for America. But she said that audiences are willing to show glimmers of sympathy and understanding for almost anyone onscreen *except* a character who is mean to animals. One man's terrorist is another man's freedom fighter. Sexual attraction to children? Maybe the perpetrator was abused himself. But kick a dog, and be cinematically damned. And the poor actor required to kick (okay, *mime* kicking) a dog on-screen will statistically have limited luck getting cast afterward in "good guy" parts. I'd list some of these luckless big-screen dog-kickers, but you wouldn't recognize their names. Unlike people who have sex with underage children (remember *Roman Polanski*?), committing animal cruelty on-screen is a career-killer.

"Kick the dog" as a character trope was first institutionalized in the early Hollywood westerns. Three bad guys ride into town. The first guns down the sheriff, the second kills his deputy, the third kicks a dog. Guess which one the hero shoots first? The cinematic corollary to "Kick the dog" is "Pat the dog," an action deployed to make audiences warm to characters of dubious moral fiber. ("Pat the kitty," by the way, sends the opposite message — think Mike Myers's Dr. Evil or James Bond's Blofeld — kitty-patters are straight-up freaks.) The idea being, a bad guy who pauses in his villainy to pat a dog can't be all bad. "Pat the dog" signals his potential for redemption. And though he's seldom redeemed, the hint of dog-loving adds depth and nuance to his character, and ensures our regret when he dies.

"Shoot the dog," ironically, is a trope reserved for heroes. "Shoot the dog" happens when a beloved canine (think Old Yeller) contracts a horrific disease, and dog-killing can be framed as human sacrifice of the highest order. However, unlike Old Yeller, my Precious wasn't conclusively facing an imminent and excruciating death. She hadn't lost her mind, or reverted to the mouth-foaming savagery that made her a danger to herself and others. She was covered with lesions and had a presumptive tumor on her brain, which might not have killed her for months. Her frequent seizures were somewhat controlled by a massive daily dose of phenobarbital. Basically, she was old, incontinent, smelled bad, whined incessantly, and had become aggravatingly and expensively needy.

My killing Precious was a choice.

A callous person does the math. Weighs the difficulty of daily caretaking against years of tail-wagging, front-door greetings; a urine-scented home against the opprobrium of friends; the cumulative cost of expensive drugs and tests against a hypothetical family vacation. Even now I'm justifying, offering excuses for calling Down Dog. Does it count that I deliberated for 24 hours before deciding? Or how untroubled I was about the choice until I contemplated how I'd be judged?

3.

My defining characteristic has always been a tendency to run headlong toward things that scare me. I suspect this is a mis-wiring of my primal fight-or-flight response: if something's unknown or can hurt me, I move *toward* it rather than away. Friends choose to perceive this as "fearlessness," (a flattering notion) but in truth, the way I manage fear is to hurl myself at the scary situation and see if I can survive. This ability to override the most basic of instincts comes down to the completely irrational notion that *risk=reward*. Go *toward* the burning building, the sound of gunfire, the thing that might unmake you! What possesses a person to follow such illogic?

A recent brain study at Caltech suggests the culprit is curiosity. Apparently our desire for abstract information stimulates the caudate, a region of the brain directly linked to the dopamine "rewards" pathway. Curiosity begins as a dopaminergic craving, something only satisfied via a neurologic brain trip that mentally chases what we don't know. We get a "rush" (dopamine release) when curiosity transports us from ignorance to enlightenment.

In some of us, though, this curiosity outweighs caution. Or perhaps we are dopamine junkies. I attribute my counterintuitive flight-*toward*-fight to an overwhelming need to know, at any cost. Not a charming trait.

For several years I taught writing in a maximum security prison where I got to know a 19-year-old "thrill killer" (let's call him "Daniel") who'd murdered a stranger when they were both 15. Four years after the fact, "Daniel" was still bemused by his own actions. He confessed he hadn't been angry, threatened, or sexually stimulated, he'd simply wanted to know what it felt like to end a life. "Curiosity," he told me, "that's *why* you kill the cat."

4.

In daily life, women are offered few opportunities to kill. Despite the existence of female combat troops and police officers, our overall biological business has always been to bring forth life. Women sit our share of deathbeds and witness the passing of those we love, but how often do we deliberately end a life? (I should confess I don't consider abortion to be "killing" because I've had one. The procedure took place at a free clinic with protesters massed on the sidewalks. A man wearing a US Marine Corps "Death from Above" sweatshirt spit at me and angry women shouted "Killer!" Running that gauntlet was infinitely more traumatic than the D&C that followed. We can argue endlessly about the point at which cells are sufficiently mature to constitute "life," but if abortion is killing, let's call it suicide rather than murder.)

Before Precious, I'd taken a life only once — while snowed in on a remote West Virginia mountaintop with my college boyfriend. We'd survived three days on a few cans of beans found in a cupboard, but on the fourth day, both cranky from hunger, my boyfriend shot a wild turkey in the clearing outside the cabin. Plucked and roasted, it was indescribably delicious, and because we needed food, killing it was justifiable. A day later, with plenty of bird left till the snow should thaw, we shot a deer. I say "we," but there is only one finger on a trigger, and the shot was mine.

A good deer hunter aims for the heart and never takes a shot he's unlikely to make. The heart-shot promises a clean and instant kill, the animal dead before its body hits the ground. I'd never hunted before. We'd brought along the rifle purely for protection after seeing bear tracks outside the cabin that morning. I was only carrying it because my boyfriend had knelt to tie a bootlace when the deer appeared between some trees.

He was huge. A white-tailed buck with a six-point rack and haunches freckled with spots the color of the snow. The air was so sharp and cold I saw a tiny puff of smoke exit his nostrils. Spotting us he froze, perhaps equating stillness with invisibility. The moment he exhaled again I fired. It was an unthinking action, born from adrenalin and something less defensible. The bullet winged the buck in the shoulder. He wobbled, pivoted, and made a sprint for the cover of a thicket.

Shooting is uncomplicated; killing something is not. A trigger-pull is different on a gun range when the target is a paper silhouette. No matter how good that shot, there is no *frisson* of exhilaration at the realization of having done something existentially wrong. Even if you're an atheist, the choice to end another life is a fundamental usurpation of powers beyond our purview. I've always found it inexplicable that Adam and Eve paid a greater price for eating an apple than Cain did for killing a brother. Is curiosity really a greater crime than murder?

I will tell you this: taking life is a heady thing. Blasphemous and seductive. Only childbirth can compare, but it can't unmake you in the same way. Life slipping from you is not a choice you make, but a surrender.

We tracked the deer's blood and prints for what seemed like hours. After repossessing the rifle, my boyfriend stalked ahead in silence. I sensed disapproval, whether for the sloppiness of the shot or the impulsive taking of meat we didn't need. Eventually we found the buck collapsed in a snowbank, chest heaving, legs scrabbling, neck muscles corded as he tried to lift his antlered head from the ground. My boyfriend shot him in the heart. Together we dragged the carcass back to the cabin, where we trussed and hung it head-down from a tree. What I remember most is the warmth of the body and how death had rendered it boneless. The clean smell of the skin and its softness. The long, feminine eyelashes, its perfect teeth and strangely delicate hooves. No, that's not true. What I remember most is observing myself very clinically in the wake of killing something and discovering I'd become new in my own eyes.

The protocol among hunters is that the person who kills an animal must also field-dress it. My boyfriend handed me his buck knife and showed where I should slice from anus to sternum. Cutting into a body is both harder and easier than you'd imagine. Easier, because the initial piercing of flesh requires little force until you hit bone. Harder, because it takes a strong downward sawing to open the chest, and then the fluids and entrails spill out. Organs must be carved out individually to prevent the meat from spoiling, requiring your arms be thrust up inside the cavity to the elbows. The deconstruction of a body is time-consuming and bloody.

Fresh blood has an intoxicating smell — of cold metal and geraniums — and a shimmery viscosity. Its color exists in nothing else on the planet, at once vibrantly red and densely black — like garnets melted in lava — with an added sheen of buttery fat.

Statistically, women are less likely than men to faint at the sight of blood. I attribute this to monthly periods and our comfort with the fact we bleed. Blood is not a thing, but a thing we *do*. A harbinger of procreation rather than death. In this sense, we are perhaps less fascinated by blood than men, who get glimpses mainly when violence summons it forth. Or maybe I'm hiding behind generalities and statistics to avoid telling you how killing feels. Wrong, certainly. Having done something intrinsically *forbidden*, your entire body thrums with anticipation of the lightning bolt that will surely strike. You'd like to label this an adrenalin rush, but you know how those feel; you've slammed on your brakes in traffic and come within seconds of death. This is different. It shares that physical acceleration of heartbeat and respiration and the tingling of nerve endings, but lurking underneath is something else. Not adrenalin but dopamine; a rush of pure pleasure. *So this is what it feels like*, you think. Curiosity assuaged.

5.

It appears that I'm avoiding the subject of Precious, the family dog, our Rhodesian ridgeback, whose real name might have been — was — Ginger. At this point, there's no gain in insisting on anonymity, or denying it was I who chose to end her life. Arguably, the quality of that life was nonexistent. She couldn't move freely, was old, in pain, and only going to get worse. Or maybe she wanted to stay tethered to the world and us for as long as possible; would've lingered on contentedly and died in her own time. Who can say? I can only tell you what happened.

The Down Dog van pulled into the driveway. The vet stepped out, wearing a white lab coat and bright green Crocs. He handed me paperwork to sign, along with his card — magnetized — to stick on the fridge. In the kitchen he washed his hands and prepared two syringes, one to sedate and one to euthanize her. He pulled on latex gloves. Ginger and I sat on the floor with her head in my lap. Clumps of reddish fur came away in my hands as I stroked her belly. Always a sucker for the belly rub, her tail thumped the floor as delightedly as it had done since she was a pup. (I offer you this picture despite knowing that, outside cinema, "pat the dog" never makes us pardon those we've found wanting.)

The vet injected the sedative and Ginger grew drowsy. I'd originally asked permission to administer the second shot, the one that would kill her. My thinking was, having chosen this course of action, I should also bear direct responsibility for ending her life. But I couldn't. Maybe it was the sprinkle of white age spots along her flank that recalled my dappled buck. Or a tingle that someone else might have mistaken for nausea. Instead, I lifted her sleep-heavy body off my lap, and, before curiosity could rouse and gorge itself, I left the man in white to "shoot the dog."

SIMONE FORTI >
SONG OF THE VOWELS, 2009
GRAPHITE AND MARKER ON PAPER, 26 5/8 X 21 1/8"
COURTESY OF THE ARTIST AND THE BOX, LA

Even in Love

NATHALIE HANDAL

I try to tell you
there isn't a part of you missing

that even if war
has damaged you

I want to be close
to your wound

it's your heart that undresses me
when you don't touch me

it's your noise that blows open
my darkness

and maybe, I ask
(but never ask you)

the hole you fell into
is nothing

it's what remains around it
that matters

But even in love
war inhabits me

The Oranges

NATHALIE HANDAL

They were all around me
but grew heavier and heavier

until I couldn't carry them
anymore –

who can live with such weight
around the heart

who can carry a bent flame
across the night

where pieces of a moon
keep trying to declare something

to each other
but never do

who can see anything
when light is displaced

when the oranges have been taken
far away from where they belong

To Sami

Death DIONISIA MORALES

DURING BREAKFAST — while the adults sliced bread and the children wrestled for butter and jam — Klaus lost his gravitational grip on the day.

We had traveled 6,000 miles for a family vacation, and we bustled around the kitchen in our bathing suits — three generations, ages eight to almost 80 — eager to head for the beach. Then Klaus's son said, "Anne Marie is dead." The news had arrived via text the previous night and was now delivered like an afterthought. Klaus had known Anne Marie for over 50 years; she was a tether to his youth. That cut in connection sent Klaus rocketing into reverie, hurtling into space, while the rest of us continued to orbit the kitchen table.

Einstein determined that the faster you travel, the slower time runs — a mathematical relationship with astrophysical implications. But he never considered the speed of memory, a plane of motion that defies computation. Standing by the sink, Klaus looked down between his feet as if he'd dropped something and was following its descent into darkness. This was the paradox of our kitchen universe: while we pushed to feed the children, the morning slipped quickly through the hands of the clock; but as Klaus relived a lifetime in a matter of seconds, time slowed to a crawl.

Finally he lifted his head and pounded his chest with his fist and said, "Annemi, how you fought." Only then did we recognize the asynchrony of the moment. Klaus blinked at the lunches we'd packed, and seemed confused about when we'd had time to make them. Our temporal disconnect took the shape of sandwiches and sliced fruit. We downshifted, saying things like, "She lived longer than expected," and "She was hopeful to the end," trying to close the distance between us and him. It was empty talk, but it was the kind of talk that slows the pulse and brings everyone nodding in unison. The children, who seemed to sense the change in pace, ate quietly, staring at their plates.

"We have to keep moving," Klaus said, about our plans for the day or the rest of our lives or both. And we took that as a signal to gradually accelerate. For what was left of the morning, we put him at the center of the action. We found his sandals and his towel; we packed his book and his glasses. We put a hand on his shoulder each time we skated past him. Then, when the dishes were stacked and soaking, we piled into cars and picked a path to the sea. Klaus sat up front and stared straight ahead. As flashes of light and shadow patterned his face, it was impossible to know from his expression how fast his thoughts were moving relative to our speed of travel.

WHITNEY HUBBS
UNTITLED, FROM THE ONGOING SERIES, *MY OWN METAPHORS*, 2015
SILVER GELATIN PRINT, 20 X 16"
COURTESY OF THE ARTIST AND M+B GALLERY, LOS ANGELES

UNICORN DREAMS

JEREMY N. SMITH

MY COUSIN ETHAN drives a 2006 Acura TSX. "It's a company car," he tells me. "*Was* a company car. Now it's my car." He turns on the satellite radio, fiddles with the touch-screen settings. A slow percussive beat fills the vehicle. A woman's voice enters, half murmur, half moan. "This is the chill station," Ethan says. "You put this on when you pick up someone and you want them to chill."

I arrived in San Francisco last night, en route to a journalism conference in Santa Clara, and Ethan met me after dinner. This morning, when he offered to drive me to the San Carlos Caltrain station, halfway to Santa Clara, I agreed out of curiosity as much as convenience.

I'm 37 and Ethan is 34. As a teenager, he bounced around a half-dozen high schools in California before graduating from a quasi-military academy in Montana. He never went beyond a semester at community college. While I've spent the last 15 years trying to make it as a writer, Ethan has done the same as a tech entrepreneur. We live thousands of miles apart and last saw one another at my grandmother's funeral six years ago. A cousin is the closest relative who can still be a stranger to you without anyone having done anything wrong.

Ethan zips south through San Francisco toward the highway. He's a full-bodied six-foot-something, baby-faced with a shaved head hidden beneath a black baseball cap and oversized plastic blue-framed sunglasses. A kewpie doll impersonating a bodyguard.

"I have a meeting this morning in Redwood City — by the Oracle building," Ethan says. He's been selling "a little stick" — it looks like a lighter. The stick puts Android, the Google operating system, on your TV. "Smart TV," people call it. "This guy bought one. He's Filipino." Maybe he could be a reseller, Ethan thinks. "He could sell the stick to people who want to stream Filipino TV."

We enter the 101 at half past nine, joining the long tail of rush hour. Marketing the smart TV sticks provides perhaps Ethan's only steady income, but it will never be more than piecework. Much greater is the potential for Grush, the "gamified" electronic toothbrush company of which he is one of two cofounders. With a Grush brush, now in prototype, kids can see video replicas of their mouths on any smartphone when they brush their teeth. They get points and advance levels, as in a video game, for cleaning thoroughly. It's the kind of product that seems ridiculous until, seemingly overnight, everyone uses it, like Netflix, or Airbnb, or Uber, all "unicorns"— the tech industry term for a startup valued at a billion dollars or more.

I own an electronic toothbrush. And I have a four year old. Who am I to say my cousin won't hit it big?

Ethan tells me he's trying to get Grush on *Shark Tank*, ABC's reality television show about business startups. When he finishes with the Filipino guy, he'll complete the show application packet and edit his audition video with new testimony from a Harvard-educated dentist turned company consultant. Then he'll move on to another Redwood City startup, his virtual reality headset maker: ImmersiON-VRelia. "We might change the name," Ethan says. Today. "I have to do a marketing plan."

Early afternoon, post–marketing meeting, Ethan will work out and shower at the nearby Jewish Community Center. "Then I'll see Sebastian, if he's available." Sebastian is Ethan's 12-year-old son. He was a surprise to everyone in our family, Ethan included, when we learned of his existence a decade ago. I'm sure Sebastian's mother has a name, but I have never heard her referred to as anything other than "Sebastian's mother."

Ethan runs down the rest of today's schedule.

Mid-afternoon: "I'm meeting a guy who's going to help me manage a crowdfunding campaign I'm doing for a gaming console."

Late afternoon: "I'll call this girl to talk about this Uber-of-whatever idea I have."

Tonight: "Dinner at the Palace of Fine Arts with the director of procurement at Tesla."

At my request, he explains what's at stake in each meeting. The guy he's seeing mid-afternoon is pushing the idea of a crowdfunding "smart queue," where people who talk or tweet the most about the product they're helping fund get it before other early backers. The woman he's calling afterward heads a company that offers in-home facial treatments. Ethan's "Uber-of-whatever" idea would be a software platform for her or any other service: tour guides, say, or dog grooming. Like Uber, the ride-hailing app, you'd press a button on your phone, see the total price in advance, and the service would meet you wherever you were within minutes, with automatic online payment upon completion. "I kind of want to bring her into the company," Ethan says of the facialist and his theoretical third or fourth startup. "I don't want it to be serious, though. My work is already stressful."

And dinner? Ethan tells me the Palace of Fine Arts in San Francisco, originally built for the 1915 Panama-Pacific Exposition, now hosts a tech incubator with organized talks like tonight's with the electric car company procurement chief. "It doesn't have anything to do with what I'm doing," he says, "but the food is usually good."

In the car, Ethan gnaws a strip of teriyaki tuna jerky. His baseball cap advertises what he describes as an "augmented reality motorcycle helmet maker." "They're just good at raising money," Ethan tells me. "I don't know if they're going to have a proper product."

To our left, east out his window, the 101 runs alongside the Bay. I ask Ethan his take on California's drought. "It's pretty bad," he says, chewing. "I think they should bring in the water from somewhere else. Like a pipeline or a giant desalination plant. We're right on the ocean, right?" He points out Candlestick Park, where the Giants and the 49ers used to play. "They're tearing it apart," he says.

It's 9:50 a.m. As the car in front of us merges right to turn off to the San Francisco airport, we pass a billboard for a Kickstarter campaign advertising "Limitless VR Wearability."

Ethan grimaces. "I can't believe it," he says. "That's one of our main competitors. We were talking to them about working together." Now this. "It almost makes me drive off the road."

Head shaking, he swallows the last of the jerky. "That's how it is. You have a cool idea. But then all these competitors jump in. They all want a part of it."

The billboard showed someone wearing what looked like a gas mask plugged into an iPhone. What do these virtual reality devices *do*? I ask Ethan.

"You put it on and you feel like you're somewhere else," he says. Imagine a truly 3-D movie. "You can look around or behind the scene. You can walk around the set from every angle. You control your viewpoint. If there's a car chase, you feel you're in the chase."

The tech talk cheers Ethan. He asks what I'm doing at my conference. I tell him I'm moderating a panel. "I moderate a lot of panels," Ethan says. "The trick is to get two people to argue." He tells me another trick: join a foreign press association; it costs less than $100 and, with the ID, you can get into almost any conference for free. "A lot of times, the stuff they give away at vendors' booths is pretty nice."

At 10 a.m., the Filipino guy texts to check in. We're six minutes from my train station, according to the Acura's built-in GPS system. Ethan gestures dismissively at the car's readout screen. "That's 2006. I've got to update it."

We discuss wearable devices. Ethan has one to measure his heartbeat and sleep patterns, he says. But it can't tell if you have cancer, I point out, or even a common cold. "Can't dogs detect cancer now?" Ethan asks. I don't think so, I say. He shares his big public health idea: "Spray vaccines at concerts."

Traffic slows. Cars bunch up between a red-clay-tile-roofed Marriott and the offices of Salesforce.com. I hear the chill station clearly for the first time since we entered the highway. "They call this the Oracle mile," Ethan explains. "It's always bad the mile before you get to Oracle."

A police cruiser scoots next to us. "Luckily, I got my car registered yesterday," Ethan says.

It occurs to me that, like Ethan, Larry Ellison, the cofounder of Oracle, never graduated from college. Neither did Steve Jobs, or Bill Gates, or Facebook's Mark Zuckerberg. Another billionaire tech entrepreneur, Peter Thiel, the cofounder of PayPal, graduated from Stanford and Stanford Law School, but has become famous recently for encouraging students to drop out, offering $100,000 scholarships to young people who start companies instead of seeking a degree. I ask my cousin if he feels like not having gone to college is actually an *advantage* in Silicon Valley.

"Well …," Ethan entertains the question. "It's cheaper." He chuckles with embarrassment. "If I applied for regular jobs, it would matter." And some of ImmersiON's technology partners are funded by the Chinese government. "When we apply for grants, my colleagues tell me to make up a college." He shrugs. "Maybe I'll take some online classes and get at least an AA degree. They're still kind of expensive. If they had free ones …" His voice trails off, a little wistful. "I don't have any debts," he says.

He lives in the Mission, in a free room in an apartment sublet by his father, my uncle Steve. Steve breaks even, though, by having three other renters. "Three roommates," says Ethan, "is too many for one bathroom." We pass Oracle's offices. "They're built to look like disk drives," he tells me. Traffic speed increases. Two minutes later, we're off the highway and onto city streets.

Does *he* think he'll get rich doing what he's doing?

"People have been saying to me, the past 10 years, 'Oh, you're going to be a millionaire,'" Ethan says. "I get desensitized. I own shares in all these companies. On paper, they could be worth a lot.

But I don't make much money." Grush is currently trying to raise $1 million, one-thousandth of a billion dollars. That the funding would mean giving up some of his equity doesn't bother Ethan. "If that happens, I'll have a salary," he says. "But investors look for any reason not to give."

Everything helps. "We raised $80,000 for Grush — $50,000 through crowdfunding," Ethan says. They've been written up by the BBC, *The New York Times*, *USA Today*, and *Wired*. "We're going to be on the *Steve Harvey* show. Steve Harvey is going to brush his teeth with it." And Philips and Colgate have "pursued" them, he claims. But moving from prototype to factory production is a major hurdle. "We'll see. We're just two guys doing it and I have three other jobs. My partner's concern is that if we don't do it, we won't have any credibility. We won't be able to do anything with anyone ever again."

I think of the Faulkner line about a business venture that, if it succeeded, would make its founders millionaires. And if it didn't, everyone would have to change his name and move to Texas. These days, he would have said billionaires. And Bangalore could probably stand in for Texas. Starving artists get all the attention, but there are at least as many starving entrepreneurs.

We pull into the train station at 10:15 a.m. Ethan asks if I know how to get to my hotel once I get off at the other end. I show him printed transit directions. He squints, disbelieving, and speaks into his phone: "Ok Google." He tells the machine my destination and asks for new directions, based on my specific time of arrival, which I write down. "And you can always get an Uber," Ethan says. "Call me if you need help."

He drives off down El Camino Real.

THE GIRL, THE MAN, AND THE WOMAN

FIRST CHAPTER FROM "PABLO!" A NOVEL

JOHN RECHY

LARB IS PROUD to publish the compelling first chapter of an early "lost" novel by John Rechy. He wrote it when he was 18, a decade before the appearance of his now-classic *City of Night*. The chapter shows a precocious author playing masterfully with the kinds of myths that are foundational for ancient cultures. The title character, however, does not show up yet — Pablo will be a Boy whom the Girl encounters in the Yucatan jungle, where he escapes from a possessive plantation owner after being picked up off a Mexico City street. Pablo wants to be a great dancer, and at one point he exuberantly shouts his own name, hence "Pablo!" — which is the only name in the novel as well as the only exclamation mark. The book also features talking snakes and agoutis (returned spirits), La Llorona searching for her severed head in the night, and an ancient witch who foretells only disaster. Rechy introduces the chapter from *Pablo!* and details the book's entertaining publishing history below.

~

I wrote Pablo! *when I was 18, and then during the next two or so years attempted to revise it but never did. That was not really my first novel, which was one I started years earlier. It was titled* Time on Wings *— set during the French Revolution and sympathetic to Marie Antoinette (or, more specifically, to Norma Shearer). Unfortunately I dramatically destroyed that masterpiece when I went into the army — a clean slate.*

I have no idea where Pablo! *came from. I set it in the Yucatan jungle and Mexico City (places I'd never been), framed by Mayan myths that I'd read — probably from a book left open on a public library table. I showed the original version to my dear friend Wilford Leach (the famous theater director who was then in the army in El Paso), and he sent it to his agent, who, according to him — I never saw the actual letter, he might have wanted to be kind — said I was clearly very talented, but that this book would not be fair to me, etc. She said the book contained "everything but the kitchen sink." I went into the army, and, when released, I moved to New York, planning to go back to college. I applied to Pearl Buck's Columbia University writing course. (Years later I was invited to teach the same course, but I got the semesters wrong — spring/winter — and so never did.) Buck wrote back claiming to be impressed but saying she didn't think she was "right" for me.*

Pablo! *did get me into Hiram Haydn's class at the New School. By that time I was working on a new novel,* The Witch of El Paso. *I sent* Pablo! *to Grove Press — at the time Barney Rosset was publishing a quarterly called* Evergreen Review *— and it was summarily rejected. I put a classified ad in* The New York Times *— "veteran, just released from army, recorded court-martials" — and I got a lot of calls on the hall telephone in an apartment building known as "The Casbah of 34th Street," where I had a room. One of the calls was from a publisher of a huge-circulation magazine. I met him for coffee and happened to mention* Pablo! *He'd love to see it, he said, might I want to drop it by his office? Oh, I did, I did. He called to say he'd read it and wanted to see me; he gave me an address, which turned out to be a two-story apartment on Park Avenue. He quickly got down to his real interest — me — and he wouldn't give* Pablo! *back until I mentioned that he'd never asked how old I was and that I was not yet 18 (a lie) and the doorman had seen me. I left the man, who looked like a frog, with my manuscript under my arm.*

Then City of Night *came out, and my editor remembered* Pablo! *from years back and wanted to see it again. He recommended it for publication by Grove, but I said no because it would be perceived as my "second novel" riding on* City of Night, *unfair to both. I sent the manuscript to Black Sparrow Press, and the publisher said yes, but he wanted a full revision. That would not be the book I wrote. In the meantime, the Mugar Memorial Archives at Boston University purchased the typescript of* City of Night. *Eventually I donated the manuscript of* Pablo! *to them, for retirement.*

Years later, I received the Luis Leal Award from UC Santa Barbara — finally I was acknowledged as the "Chicano" I had always been, even though "they" (Chicano "activists") wouldn't let me be, but that's another epic. The award ceremony included a fancy dinner at which my partner (now my mate/spouse), Michael, sat across the table from the highly esteemed Professor Francisco Lomeli. Michael mentioned Pablo!, *saying it was based on Mayan legends — and that it was framed by the sad love of the moon for the sun. Professor Lomeli said he would love to see it. I "borrowed" it back from Boston and sent it to him. He was excited and wrote a terrific introduction to it, placing me in the early tradition of magical realism. He sent* Pablo! *along with his introduction to Arte Público. I was offered a good advance and a not-so-good contract that my agent sniffed at — all subsidiary rights signed away Forever. So I withdrew it.*

Now that my latest book Island! Island! *(another exclamatory title, a coincidence, not a fetish) is finished and ready for publication, I will explore, with my agent, probably small prestigious presses or university presses for publication, with, of course, Professor Lomeli's glowing introduction.*

> And the soul must wander
> aimlessly until the sun and
> the moon shall fuse.
>
> — Mayan Legend

The Girl, the Man, and the Woman

1

"It is the Xtabay."

The old man squinted to see through the rain.

"It is the Xtabay," repeated the frightened voice of his wife huddled behind him. "It is she who lures men with her unholy beauty." She crossed herself and recited a prayer, unaware of the rain wetting her.

And her memory sang the words of the evil Xtabay, and she could almost hear the illusive voice calling like music played by the wind on trees,

> "Tuux ca bin?
> Coten uayé …"

beckoning the old man to come to her, luring him as she had lured others to their death,

> "Where are you going?
> Come with me …"

"It is only a girl who is lost and has fainted," said the old man. "It is not an evil spirit. I would feel it." For once in a village far away he had been a holy man, and he was warned of evil as others are warned of rain. "We must help her."

"She is pretending sleep to lure you." The woman's voice was hardly audible over the rain. "Say a prayer and leave her," the old woman demanded. The sharp claws of her ancient hands would not release her husband's arm.

And as the man proceeded toward the form of the girl encompassed by the fantastic of the plants, he mumbled something and crossed himself.

The old woman remained behind, clasping her bony hands. From the distance she saw her husband kneel before the girl, and fear enveloped her like a shroud. She took a step forward. The earth would open and swallow the man. She would hear the wicked laughter of the beautiful Xtabay, then the mocking song mingling with the sound of the rain.

But none of this happened. She saw, instead, the old man lift the girl in his arms, saw him walk back with her, still asleep or fainted deceptively, pretending whichever she wanted.

"She has fainted from exhaustion," said the man as he approached the livid old woman trembling with religious fear.

"No," said the woman, moving back frantically as the body was brought closer to her. "You do not understand. Her beauty hides … evil." As she moved farther back, she watched the face of the girl in fascination, and she understood why men were lured so easily to their destruction. This young girl in her husband's arms, evil as she was, was as beautiful as the flower of the Tzacam, into which she converted herself after bringing unholy death to men.

"If it were the Xtabay, I would feel it in my heart," said the man who in a village far away had been a holy man.

"But the face — the body," persisted the woman in an awed whisper, "they could destroy even a holy man such as you."

The man walked into the house with the girl. The wife followed a distance behind.

Inside, the sound of the rain was unreal, ominous, and the woman crossed herself again as she hurried to the corner of the one room, where the live skeleton of an ancient woman shrouded with brown skin crouched. It was the mother of the wife.

The man laid the girl gently in the hammock.

"She is very wet," he said solemnly to his wife. "Take her clothes."

The woman only retreated farther into the corner, cringing on the floor beside the fading skeleton shrouded in the horrible brown skin, thin enough that the bones were visible. And they were stark and white. The wife clung to her mother, pressing herself against the disintegrating body, clasping at the torn clothes, so that the two old women were like desiccated eagles feeding on each other.

"He has brought the evil woman into this house," the man's wife whispered to the skeleton of her mother. "He has brought the Xtabay inside."

The mother stared fixedly before her. Her eyes were covered by a thin white mist, and she never blinked. She heard only one word through the vortex of her timedestroyed mind, and that word whirled around and around, and it echoed, "Xtabay." She would have raised one terrified trembling hand, but her mind stopped thinking suddenly and she remained silent.

When the man saw that his wife would not come, he began to remove the girl's clothes. He stopped abruptly, turning away. The ancient hand touched the smooth flesh of the girl's arm. Quickly, he withdrew it. He gazed at the face, at the closed eyes, the black hair moist on the beautiful face. He turned away fiercely, avoiding the beauty of the girl.

On the hammock, the girl was breathing audibly. She could hear the soft rain even in the stupor into which she had fallen. She heard the thunder, once, and it burst loudly in her mind and then entered the realm of silence. She spun toward unconsciousness, into the world of pure motion.

"Look, he is lost, he cannot move, she has paralyzed him, he is lost to the evil Xtabay." The wife's voice rose hysterical and insane. She embraced the skinshrouded skeleton beside her.

Once again, the name reverberated in the mother's ears, and, her mind clinging to the word this time, she began to chant from the wasteland of her memory the legend of the beautiful Xtabay, to chant like a priest the words long buried in her mind, confusing her own life with the life of the other, the hungry hunter of her tale.

"She who lures all men … Searching until time ends for physical love — searching in death because in life she denied the spiritual … To fill her empty yearning." She chuckled mirthlessly. "Lost — …" she breathed. "Lost searching a substitute for salvation …" Then she trembled, as if completely alive again. "And I became a flower full of thorns … But the Xkeban, my sister, who loved in life smells of beauty."

The old man retreated from the hammock, and in a moment he returned to cover the girl's body. He who was a holy man, who was very, very old — and closer now to the spirits and the great god, he who had even denied his wife to remain pure — he had almost surrendered to the evil of desire.

"And the man saw her standing at the door, and he let her in, for it was raining," the wheezing voice of the mother continued. "My father, who is dead, the Xtabay lied … but he did not believe her, for he recognized the luring, sweet voice of evil … For all evil is sweet … And as he held me in life — before my wandering death — I strained to reach his young body, not his soul, and then it came to me like a god … And he burned a strand of her hair and buried the ashes, to keep the evil from him …"

For the first time, the wife became aware of the mother's voice. And remembering the ancient charm, she stared at the girl's long hair.

The girl opened her eyes. She felt the woman's hatred. But she closed her eyes again quickly because this was the world of reality, of unrealized desire.

"You are lost," the old man told her softly, crushing the evil within him. "And I will help you find your way, wherever it is."

She opened her mouth, concentrating on the words she must form. Finally she was able to whisper, "To the great place ... the great modern city of the Mexican people ..." And in that instant she saw lightning lash at the sky, and the lightning became the lithe, supple whirling body of a boy of desperate eyes. She called his name. Then there was no lightning, and the turbulent body was gone.

When the old man was certain that the girl would speak no more, he went to his wife, his head lowered. The memory of the sin still scorched him. He must vindicate himself, he was too close to god.

"When the girl wakes," he told his wife, whose face was contorted by fear, "I will take her wherever she will want to go."

His wife shrieked unintelligibly at him as she clung to the starkwhite bones of her mother.

On this side of the house, the ground was moist but dry enough to sustain a fire, for the rain fell lightly and obliquely. The wife of the man who in a faraway village had been holy stood looking down at the ground, her fists clenched.

In one hand, she held something black.

She knelt on the ground, laying beside her what she had held in her fist — and it was a long strand of the girl's hair. The old woman dug into the earth with her hands, and triumph was written on the hollowcheeked face. When she had finished digging, she made a fire on the ground, and ceremoniously, aware of her affinity to good, she burned the girl's hair. In a moment there was nothing left but a small pinch of ashes. She collected them carefully and dropped them into the hole, covering it quickly.

As she walked into the thatched house, the claws of her hands were buried into her flesh, cutting.

In a village far away, the father of the girl stared at the clouded sky. The rain fell in scattered drops.

About him, in the surrounding milpas a distance away where the corn would be grown, smoke rose in gray clouds. The other villagers had banded together, rushing from field to field to burn the brush that must be burned before the planting of the maize. But the father of the girl was alone. And it was perhaps too late to fire the brush in his field — had been too late even as he had stood at the entrance to the village returning to his house to find his daughter gone.

Like the others, he had watched the skies daily for a sign, and he had watched the brush, still green, knowing that he must wait until it was dry enough to burn. Now the rain had come unexpectedly, and the long hours in the field cutting the brush, digging with his bare hands for the groundclutching roots, would be wasted.

From a distance very far — above the sound of the burning brush, the cracking fire struggling against the erratic rain, over the sound of stamping feet of men rushing with flaming tahche in hand — the man heard the words of supplication to the ancient deities of the field and the mysterious Catholic god, and he heard the doleful voice of one of the elders of the village forming the words almost forgotten by a new generation of milperos,

"Cu yantal in kubic le zaca ti nohol ik yetel ti
kakal-mozonkanik ..."
"To the south wind and the furious whirling wind,
offer this zaca ..."

Now the trembling hand would be thrusting the corn into the air, that suddenly the rain would stop and the friendly wind would blow across the land carrying the fire across the fields, all this before the storm came smothering the fire and soaking the bushes, rendering the fields useless for the planting.

"To the east wind also, so to the four corners of my
field ..."

The father of the girl stood like one dead with open eyes, and the only sign of life was the perspiration that covered his face, his arms, his legs. But he did not feel this, or the steamy heat — felt only the sadness of the impending ruin of his field and the greater loss of his daughter.

"To the north, to the west, to the south winds also,
so to the great god father and the sainted lord archangel ..."

And standing so, aware of the crushing power of something which he hated and could not understand, he seemed to have sprung from the violent soil. His face was dark brownred, like the land itself, and like the land it was harsh, strong, violent.

And that harshness and violence were clearly in every part of him, in the hair, which was coarse and dark, in the eyes, which were black, in the strong body.

"In the name of god the father, of god the son, of god the holy ghost, amen," ended the lugubrious chant of the elder.

And the rain stopped.

And the father of the girl who was gone looked up into the sky, very long, and then, with resuscitated hope, he was running swiftly toward his own field, the tahche in his hand — the long stick to fire the brush. He ran unstopping for a long time, and then he was standing in his field. At various places his legs were cut by the thorny plants of this country.

The ground about him was unhallowed, and great pleasure surged through him at the realization, and he breathed furiously. No holy hmenob had prayed over it, no altar had been erected to the field gods, no zaca offered to the spirits of his milpa. He had defied the spirits, the holy chaacs and balams, and the rain had stopped, and he could win again — could still burn the brush. Life pounded violently in him, as it had earlier, the months before when he had searched greedily for the fertile land, where the palms heralded the excellence of this soil, surged through him as it had when he had cleared the land, attacking each tree with the small ax as if he were slaying the spirits of the ancient gods whom he hated, digging out the roots, ripping the earth, attacking nature, and defying the god.

The raised tahche in his hand was flaming, and he was running across the field. The fire passed from the pole of catzim wood to the crying trees and bushes. Smoke ascended. The wood began to sputter, and then to crack — and then the fire came alive, roaring, and the flames whirled openjawed and embraced the land.

And then the sky burst open, and the rain came pouring.

It fell over the fire, hissing, soaking the scorched earth, the brush, and very soon the flames were gone, and only the mocking sight of smoke remained.

And the rain released the heat of the soil that rose like a judgment in furious waves of steam.

The house of the man was farther from the others than is usual. It was like all the others, of poles interlacing, of mud plaster, of green covering.

The father of the girl saw the house, and he thought of the woman who would be inside, and he thought of his field, soaked useless.

He walked into the house.

The rain had entered at various places. Streaks of dark light lined the floor and spilled into the water that had gathered. It was almost barren, this house of the one room, like the others in the village. From the ceiling the peten hung dismally, now wet, in which the food was kept. Against the walls were the metate for the grinding of the maize, and the baskets, the small bench, the hammock.

He turned away quickly from the hammock. But his eyes returned involuntarily. And as if the memory had buried a knife in his heart, he remembered the girl who was gone.

Urgently, he turned to face his wife.

She knelt facing him on the floor, the hands lying one on the other as if she had been praying. The face was solemn. The skin over the skull seemed so tight that laughter appeared impossible, as if it would rend the skin. It was a thin face, inscrutable, mysterious.

It was only the eyes that gave her life — long and slanted and very, very deep. It was they that showed emotion, and they laughed now triumphantly.

Her hair was braided tightly into one braid that coiled like a thick snake at the nape of her neck. She was dressed in immaculate white which clung to the slim body. Her feet were bare.

The man stared at his wife, into the abysmal eyes.

The eyes burst into greater laughter. They mocked, boasted of her triumph and of his defeat. The face was solemn.

Anger seared him. Her eyes were a mirror of the past months, and he saw himself under the blazing sky digging into the earth. Desperately, he turned away from her and sought again the empty hammock. Again, he faced the woman. He stood over her, his body so tense that his legs began to bleed from the thorny cuts.

He pulled her up with both hands. He shook her so violently by the shoulders that the braided snake coiled at her neck unwound its body and hung limply the length of her back.

"Laugh," he shouted.

But the face did not move. It remained a mask which only tearing can change.

He struck the mask. Still, it did not change. The despised eyes continued to laugh and boast. He struck her again, trying to make the face cry, to destroy the depthless gaze. Her lips bled — but the eyes were unchanged.

Then she fell to the ground, at his feet. She opened her mouth, and the blood gushed out like a shapeless animal.

Standing over her, he shouted, "You have been praying — for this."

The strange eyes smiled.

"And you won," he said dully.

"They won," she said.

"Your gods," he said.

The eyes laughed.

"And the field is destroyed — lost — months, long long months," he said. "And the girl — she is gone too. Forever."

"I have prayed," she said softly. "I have prayed for the destruction of your field. And I have prayed for the boy that has taken her from you. And now there will be vindication for the sin."

Helpless fury flashed through him, helpless because no matter what he did she was the victor. "And even as I was in the field, even as the sun — even then, you were praying."

"Yes," she said. "I have prayed for your destruction."

Anger burst into passion, lust and hatred becoming one, both demanding gratification. He longed to conquer her, to hurt and destroy her, as she had destroyed him — and yet suddenly he longed even more to make her a part of him, to dispel in that way the unbearable loneliness inside him, to make her feel the loss as he felt it, to make her understand as he understood.

His breath came in spasms now, and something beat in his head louder than the rain outside.

He knelt before the woman.

He put his hands gently inside the immaculate dress, drawing it easily from her breasts.

She didn't move.

He called her name softly, with something more than tenderness, something which not only demanded but pled urgently. Still, she did not respond, and his hands moved over her body.

"I want you," came his choked words. "I want you, like on that night, so long ago —"

"No," she whispered quickly, and there was the barest echo of emotion in her voice, and the face seemed alive suddenly. But the mask covered it again, and the stoical voice said, "She is gone now, gone forever now to seek the boy."

"I want you," he repeated.

"My body, my flesh."

His arms were wet, his whole body was wet with the rain and the perspiration as he raised her in his arms. He felt himself bursting with power, and his fingers dug into her flesh as he had dug for the roots in the ripped earth of his field. He placed her on the ground and knelt over her.

And as he took her violently, she remained like one long dead.

ARTIST PORTFOLIO

MILJOHN RUPERTO AND RINI YUN KEAGY

ORDINAL (SW/NE) is a film in progress. It takes place in Bakersfield, a city in California's Central Valley that is a center of agricultural production.

The film overlays two systems of thought: geomancy and agrilogistics. Geomancy (at least as presented here) is a kind of divination, or a way of organizing the world based on aesthetics. Geomancy is an arranging principle to form auspicious structures; it is superstitious architecture. Agrilogistics is a term promoted by philosopher Timothy Morton to describe the trajectory of human ascendancy during which humans have organized the planet to maximize food production. (This era of human ascendancy is known as the Anthropocene.) Agrilogistics is both the way the world is organized by humans and the source of human imaginings: science, religion, philosophy, aesthetics, and politics. Agrilogistics is ruthlessly efficient and totalizing.

The film examines the systems of geomancy and agrilogistics by considering several figures or ideas — dust, wind, Bakersfield, valley fever, the demon Pazuzu, Rose of Sharon from John Steinbeck's *The Grapes of Wrath*, and British filmmaker John Boorman — and their convergence.

Valley fever is a disease caused by *Coccidioides immitis*, a fungus that lives in the soil. Once unearthed, the spores ride on the wind and dust until inhaled into a host lung. They eventually settle in the ends of the bronchial alveoli, where, if unchecked, they multiply and spread throughout the body, causing illness and death. Dr. Antje Lauer of California State, Bakersfield is currently studying valley fever and appears in the film to discuss the life cycle of the cocci and how it affects individuals and the population.

Valley fever is the intersection of dust, wind, and plague. An ancient Assyrian demon, Pazuzu, also shares this axis. Pazuzu is the demon/god of the southwest wind. He brings about desolation through pestilence. He is the geomantic manifestation of valley fever. The environmental forces that Pazuzu represents — wind, dust, and disease — infiltrate the body, compromising bodily integrity, and turning the outside (i.e., the environment) in.

Terrible though he was, Pazuzu was actually utilized by some Mesopotamians to ward off another evil, Lamashtu. Lamashtu is a demon who brings death upon infants and unborn children. She was especially feared by mothers and pregnant women, who wore amulets bearing Pazuzu's visage to keep Lamashtu at bay.

UNLESS OTHERWISE NOTED, ALL IMAGES COURTESY OF THE ARTISTS AND KOENIG & CLINTON.

In John Steinbeck's *The Grapes of Wrath*, the pregnant Rose of Sharon goes westward with her family to escape the desolation of Oklahoma's Dust Bowl. A mysterious woman warns Rose of Sharon that she will lose her baby if she participates in dancing or "play actin'." While working in a field near Weedpatch Camp, just outside of Bakersfield, Rose of Sharon falls ill. Her fever causes her to go into premature labor, and she gives birth to a stillborn child. Her Uncle John places the stillborn corpse in an apple box and sends it downstream on a flood river. The Joads then take refuge in a barn where they find a young boy and his father, who is dying of starvation. The father can't eat solid food. Rose of Sharon offers the dying man her breast to suckle. The cruel Lamashtu is often depicted as a lion-headed demon holding a snake in each hand, suckling a black dog and a pig on each breast.

Pazuzu infects the contemporary world in William Peter Blatty and William Friedkin's horror film *The Exorcist*. In the film, Pazuzu possesses the body of young Regan MacNeil and battles Father Merrin and Father Karras over the soul of the child. In John Boorman's sequel, *Exorcist II: The Heretic*, Regan, now an adult, is possessed again by the plague demon.

During the filming of *Exorcist II: The Heretic*, director John Boorman inhaled *C. immitis* from dust on set in the Warner Bros. studio in Burbank, California, and contracted valley fever. Boorman was hospitalized, and shooting was suspended for a month.

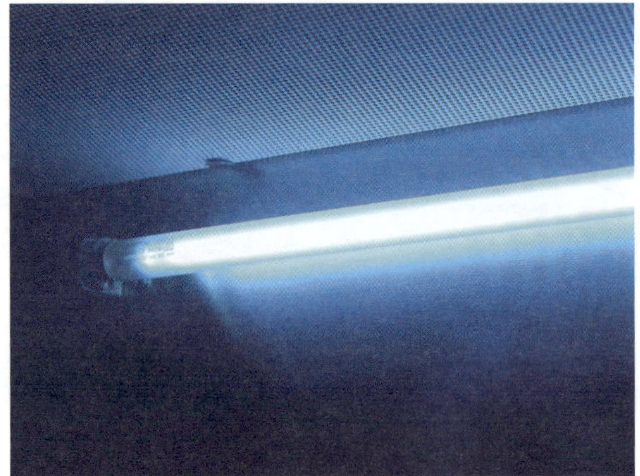

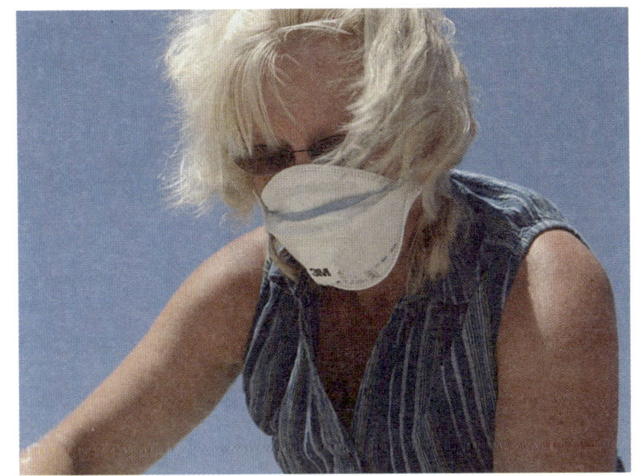
3M

SLIDE WARMER
HEAT

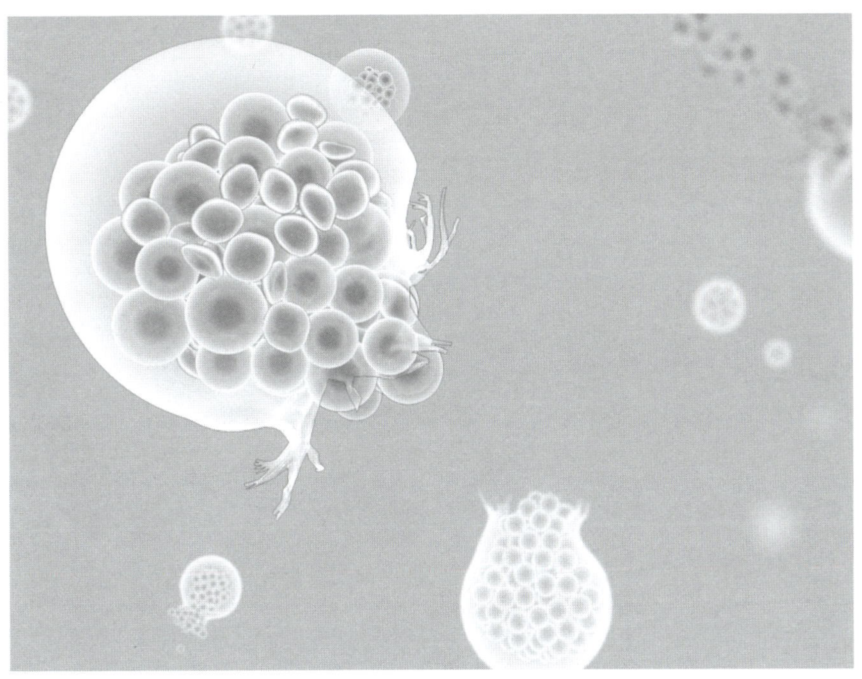

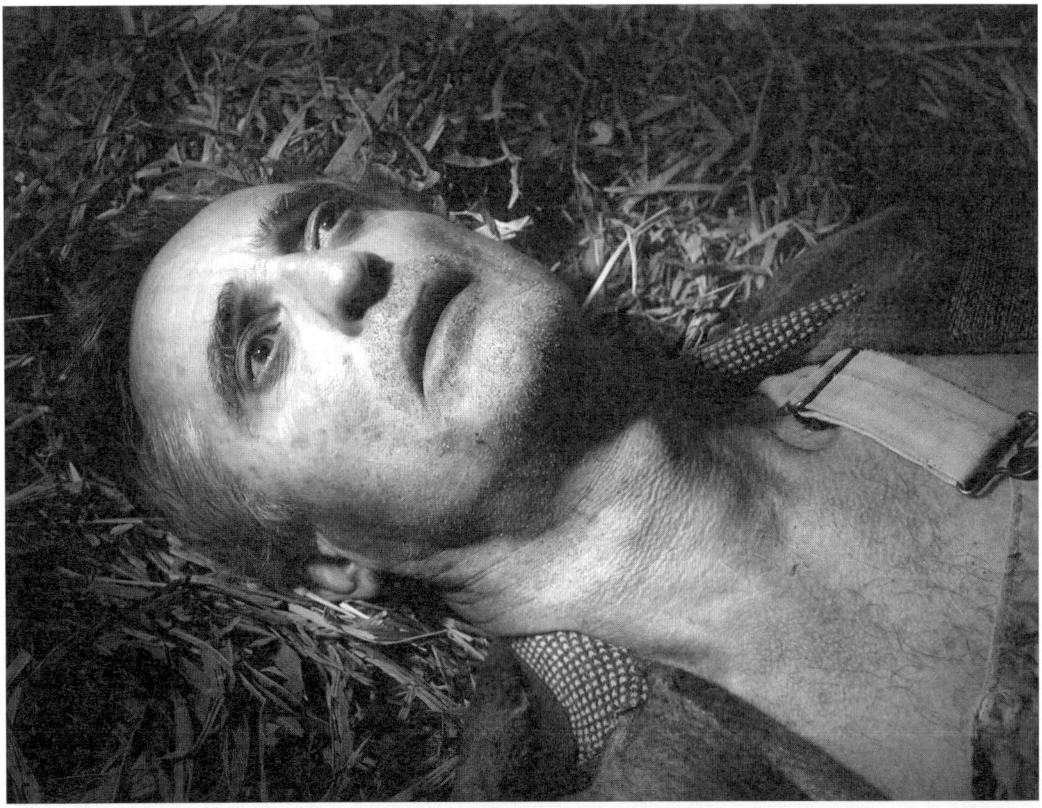

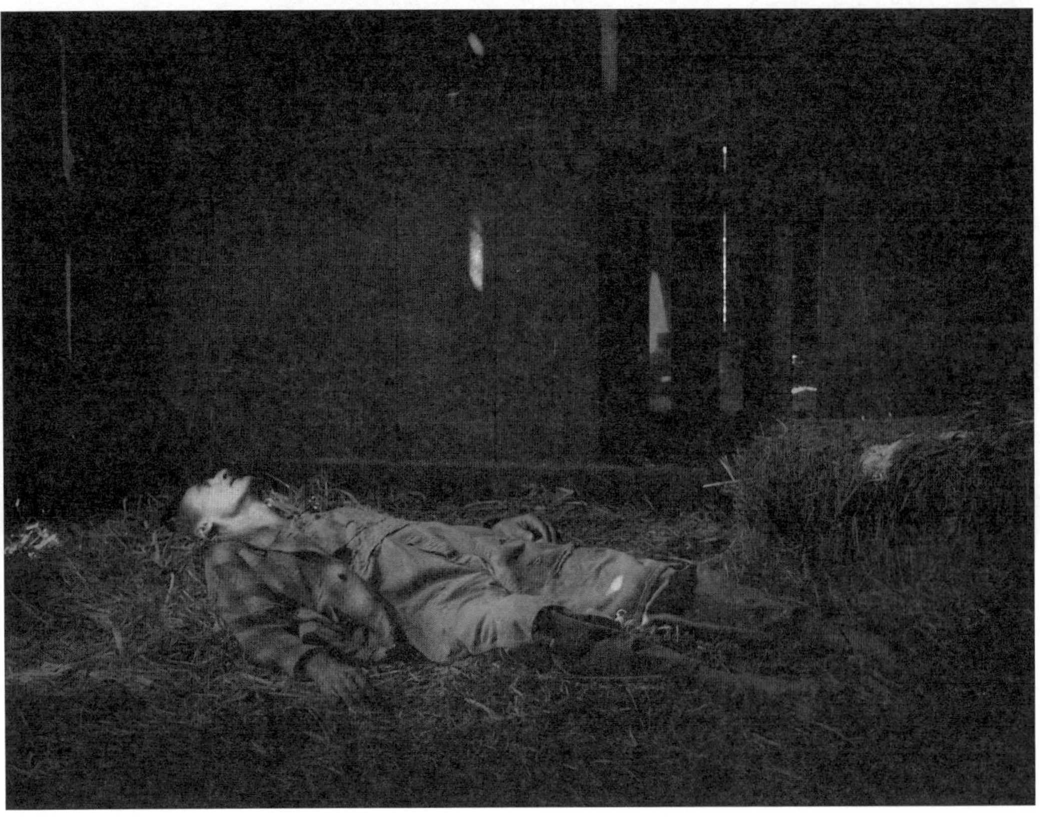

SAM CHASE, *VALLEY TURBULENCE*
THIS PHOTO WAS TAKEN NEAR ARVIN, CALIFORNIA, ON DECEMBER 20, 1977, FROM A SMALL SINGLE-ENGINE AIRCRAFT.
COURTESY OF SAM CHASE

Postcard ROBERT ANTHONY SIEGEL

FROM WENWU TEMPLE ABOVE Sun Moon Lake: we go to pay our respects to the learned master, Confucius. Red and gold everywhere, sandalwood incense, furiously praying students, a woman on her knees throwing the two wooden half-moons that foretell the future. To one side of the altar is the sort of glass-enclosed machine you would expect to find in an arcade: a little mechanical figure of a woman standing outside a miniature temple. A sign says, not only in English but in Japanese too, *The woman will bring you a poem.* I can always use a poem, so I insert a coin in the slot. Music plays (strangely great music, the pling of a Chinese harp), and the little figurine of the maiden turns around and enters the miniature temple (I'm a sucker for temples within temples) and then comes out again carrying a miniature scroll, which she drops into the slot. Unscrolled, it's not a poem; it's a fortune, and the English says:

> To make new plans for the continuing of litigation.
> To mark out new plans for securing both fame and wealth.
> Travelers be hindered.
> To examine character with a view toward reformation.

I stand there feeling transparent. ... Suddenly it starts to pour outside, a rain so intensely muscular the lake and mountains beyond the gate disappear, as if the gods had pulled shut a curtain. And so we really are in a poem.

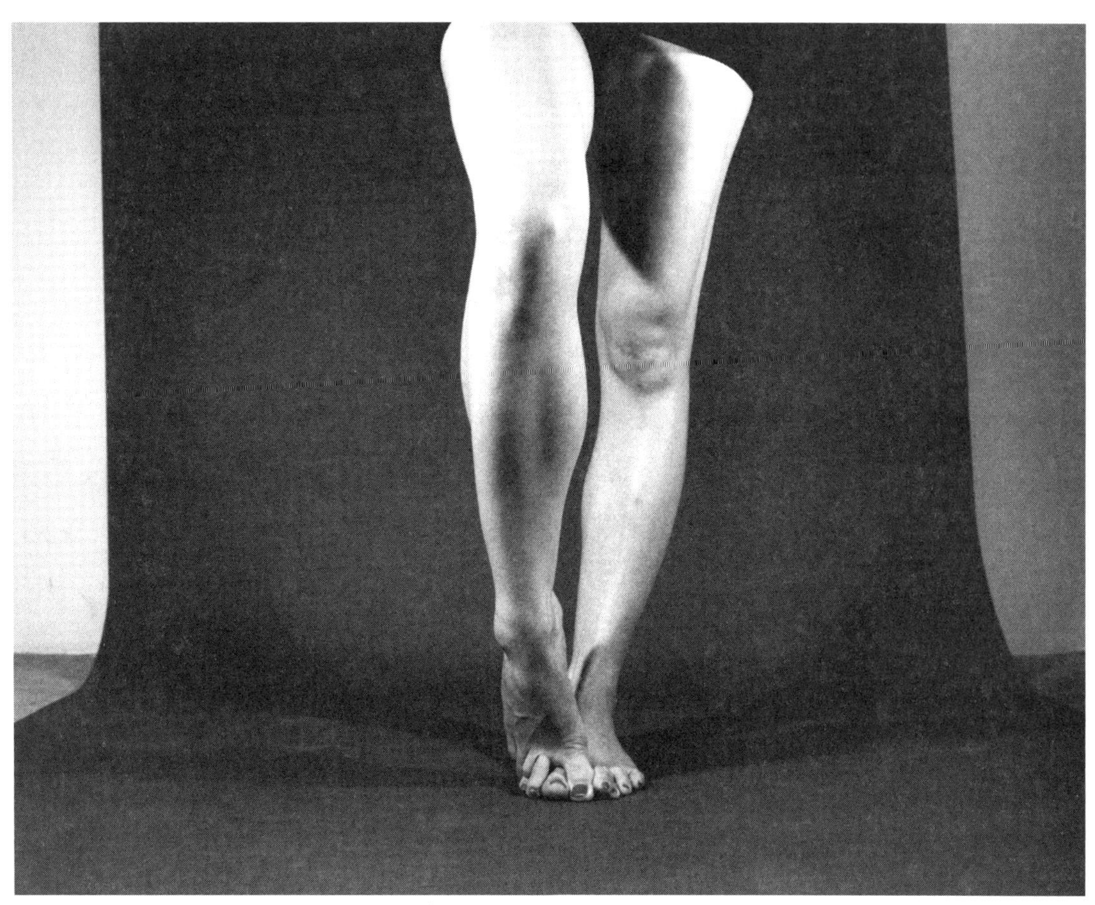

WHITNEY HUBBS
UNTITLED, FROM THE ONGOING SERIES, *MY OWN METAPHORS*, 2015
SILVER GELATIN PRINT, 16 X 20"
COURTESY OF THE ARTIST AND M+B GALLERY, LOS ANGELES

A PLAY BY MAC WELLMAN

ANGELA WOODWARD

AS I CROSSED West Wash heading home on my bike, a parade of marchers, accompanied by or held back by mounted police, came toward me on one side, and from the other direction, a freight train. The bike path ran parallel to the tracks. While the parade or protest flashed behind me, I ran on alongside the train for a few more seconds, until I came to the point where the tracks and the path intersected. I stopped and waited for the train to pass with everyone else. No one spoke to me. We straddled our bikes, feet on the ground, leaning on the handlebars, three or four of us in the front row only a few feet from the train. It barreled on and on, its graffiti flickering past — crazy letters and symbols, whole cartoons, girls kissing, Popeye, a man in a hat, funny, articulate, vivid human faces. The horn blasted. The wheels screeched. The high-pitched metal on metal scraped and rattled repetitively. The faces and letters ratcheted by like frames of a movie, the noise like a soundtrack at top volume, announcing the climactic scene.

Yet the climax held off. I felt caught in the acceleration and rising motion of suspense, without any standard narrative relief: the fist hitting the chin, the lips joining each other, the thud of corpse onto sand, the last look dissolving into distance, or a note descending a step to resolve the chord. If this were a movie or a symphony, I thought, it would be very boring at this point, the structure off, the timing sluggish. We should have already come to closure and then resumed the life outside the theater or the auditorium. I circled away through the crowd of waiting bikers to get a better view of the train. It stretched over the bridge around the lake in a long curve, with no end visible. I rode back to my place right at the front. No one else had moved. Still the train came on, the yellow and pink and red paint of the graffiti shining out, the ladders and couplings and hinges and latches etched in rusty brown or green or black, the wheels shrieking and grating, the ground shaking. The kind of movie or symphony this is, I thought, is like something by Guy Maddin, or some similar iconoclast genius who disdains the rising and falling arc of our expectations and instead takes the story or theme or chord progression and rams it down our throats, not stopping until so long after we've had enough that it becomes its own rare sensation, a feeling that we've abandoned our hopes of coming to a stop and walking out of the theater, that we might just drown in the sensation of the unfettered ongoingness of the sensation. The brakes screeched but didn't slow down, the train hurtled but didn't pass, like lovers who meet and make love for hours until their passion becomes another land, another way of passing time, another way of living rather than a refuge from living, another way of feeling in the body, one that doesn't wait for the next thing to come but is always coming and coming along.

It made me remember a play by Mac Wellman I'd seen in Chicago more than 20 years earlier.

It may have been set in a carnival or funhouse, with a man, a woman, and a man. The actors didn't interact with each other but spoke past and through each other in stilted lines, some in rhyme, about things they'd seen and remembered and heard about. We went on actors' night, the Monday show just for those in the business, who were at our own events on weekends. The crowd was sparse in the dingy space just down from the sprawling taqueria at the diagonal intersection of Division and Ashland. There were only six of us or so in the hard, cheap folding chairs wobbling on the risers. The actors spoke and walked around, climbing onto a box or stepping down toward a light in front. They didn't look at us, though there were so few of us it was hard to pretend we weren't there. They weren't there for our sake, it seemed. The actors' words declaimed themselves, as if the words had climbed into these actors' mouths so they could launch into the air, the actors' mouths and throats convenient vehicles for the strings of phrases. The half-lines and declarations had found a way to gather these actors on this evening so that the vowels and consonants could consort.

Anything as base as a storyline had been knifed in the alley long ago, and if the actors were listed in the program across from the names of characters, it still didn't mean that these characters were fictional imitations of people walking around. Maybe there was a "Tom" and a "Brenda" and a "Gilbert," but these were only labels for sorting the strings of phrases that issued from the actors. Like quarter notes, rests, and caesuras in a musical score, the names were notations rather than representations of specific human beings. The actors propelled the words into the air, as loudly as possible, over and past each other, a nonstop shouting that would have indicated anger or outrage if the shouting had any corresponding softer voices. But the knob was at 10 the entire time, the loudness not signaling emotion of any sort — the volume was rather a feature of the voices, like a box that could be checked, *select all: loud*. As such, it was impossible to "follow" the play, as in discerning what was happening. What was happening was the actors shouting as they ambled around their rudimentary set in front of the empty folding chairs in the darkened room down the street from the taqueria.

At one point one of the male actors, the "Tom" or the "Gilbert," stood on the box and bent his body back like a sail. "America," he indicated somehow with his string of phrases, had hung him from a branch, had left him out to dry, had let him flap, flap in the wind like a sheet on a laundry line, had hanged him from the crossbar of the mast of a sailing ship, had kidnapped and starved and neglected him but left him alive, shouting but not being heard, like a ghost at a party hovering helplessly around his widow, who he found slurping gin and tonic with another man. He had been abandoned already but he was still alive, still feeling, and that was worse than being dead. The actor was so skilled that he conveyed all these images — the lynched man, the hanged sailor, the billowing sheet, the hapless ghost — with fluid changes of his posture, also flipping from tragic to comic to tragic as easily as cricking his neck. Before, the shouting had been a unifying feature that blotted out any underlying sentiment, but here in this brief flinging of phrases from the box, sorrow and anger and pity and wonder flared out of the words and phrases, the gestures and vowels, with a palpability close to human interaction, almost conversational, like when your despairing friend calls on the phone and says nothing is wrong, then starts sobbing.

I laughed, I cried, as the critics say, at this brief spasm of splendor in the midst of untethered walking and shouting. The connection to the human was so precious because it had been slung up in between all the cardboard gangling of the abstract words and phrases. Out of all the incomprehensible emptiness came this cry, which was in itself about the emptiness, look how empty it is, this stage, and all this shouting, and how touching. That was not the climax of the play, but it was the only moment I really recalled. Walking home in the dark, sidling around the drunks outside the liquor store next to the post office and avoiding the gaping holes in the sidewalk on that busy block, my friends and I marveled at our good luck, that we had gotten to see that play in its short run.

A few days later, the review came out in the *Reader*. The critic unloaded all his bitterness and disdain at the play, which he called a mistake, a purposely bad play written to deliberately break the rules of good plays. He called the play juvenile, insulting, worthless, an affront. He took the full length of his column to detail the play's shortcomings. He seemed to have carefully researched the ways the play was bad and the author misguided, detailing his critique with precise quotations. In a week, the play folded, and more than that, the theater company that had put it on lost so much money that it went out of business. I went to work at my thankless job at American Reinsurance, where I was a temporary receptionist, steaming over the damage that critic had done with his review. I thought it was unconscionable that one review could demolish a whole theater company. I didn't know if the critic had been malicious, if he had known that his words would have their dire result. I thought of writing a response, hoping the *Reader* would publish it. I thought of writing the playwright or the director and telling them how much the play had meant to me. I could have called them on the phone — the director was a friend of friends.

I thought about all the things I should do and say and write every day when I went to work at American Reinsurance. It began to mount up on me, my tremendous responsibility for righting the wrong this critic had done. I had enjoyed the play, and now I had a duty to defend it. Every day that passed without writing a letter to the *Reader* or a letter to the playwright, without getting the phone number of the director, drove me deeper into anguish. I became no good to myself, deriding myself for being afraid, too lazy, too ineffectual to write down my thoughts and put my words to some use. You have hung me out to dry, America, I could have written, and I flap here, like a sheet, uselessly moaning: you don't love me, you don't love me at all. But I feel something, I'm alive though you've hanged me, I feel it, you, America, you. I could have said something like that. I could have done some good. I could have repaid the good faith of the playwright and the director and the actors, who had maybe lost their confidence in themselves because of what the critic had published in the *Reader*. I thought all this every day for weeks, but I didn't say or write anything, just went to work and came home.

At last the end of the train came in sight. What had seemed an infinite snake now showed itself bounded, like the rest of us. The bikers began to kick their pedals backward and get ready. Very soon there would be a time with no train in front of us, and we could ride the rest of the way home unimpeded. The last cars went by, brown, brown, green, brown, green. This train had not just one caboose to mark its endpoint, but two in a row latched together. This seemed to me superior artistry, as if the train acknowledged its grandeur and extended structure. It took two beats — caboose one, caboose two — to bring it to a close. The path cleared. All of us fit and hardy commuters whizzed off almost noiselessly. The fine whir of rubber on asphalt could not compare with the din of the train's passage. I looked back. The parade had come up the street and almost crossed the path behind us all. The brown horses framed the leading banner, which declared in

Spanish the battle cry *Venceremos*. I should have been with them, but once again I had missed the opportunity to shout and protest, to declare on this May Day our right to be noticed, to be heard. I hadn't even thought of joining them. The organizers had organized it, the kids had left their after-school clubs, the moms had skipped work to lumber up the street, hemmed in by armed men on horseback. Wouldn't I like to shout with them, "The people, united, will never be defeated"?

I haven't always kept so quiet. What was stopping me, especially now that there was nothing at all blocking the way?

PIETER SCHOOLWERTH
AFTER TROY 6, 2012
OIL, ACRYLIC, GICLÉE PRINT AND OIL PASTEL ON CANVAS; 72 1/2 X 54"
COURTESY THE ARTIST AND MIGUEL ABREU GALLERY, NEW YORK; PHOTO: JEFFREY STURGES

Broken Koan #9

WILLA CARROLL

after Dogen & Mumon

My face before the birth of my parents / an original omen /
a tragic fractal mask / slapped by old gods / a sky-written
emoticon / self-effacing / self-erasing / apocalyptic grin /
singing contralto through a red curtain / a nervous cameo /
caught by encores / a neuron hotel / a top animal / host to
microbes / expensive shelter / my neutrinos lost / my dark matter
abandoned / inside myself / guest inside guest

1st Letter to Saint Paul

JOSH BELL

This is my new home
among the people of soap, cheap
Corinthian motel
where the sun is not
the favored star, where the large birds, grown weary
of the limits of the shell, go creeping
to the bedrooms
of the featherless. When your words come,
each they come to me
down the chain, with my babies
crawling all over them, microscopic
pink algae in the seam
between testaments. The live birth.
The rational haircut. The smoke from the kidney-fires
blowing in shifts from the desert plain
and floating to me, over the motel pool
like cinema, the water tinged pink
with that grain, that babiest of algae. Places
everyone. I've got
a zip-up chest pocket meant
for a phone, but it's where I keep
an extra nipple. For trade
in prison. For loan or friendship
in the lobby. Touch it. Don't
touch it. Self-portrait
as human being.

2 Bogeys

JOSH BELL

All the living skulls in Corinth
have grown their soft spots back. On
your dashboard, one knee-high, rolled in its packaging
like black calamari. Time past
to be anything but calm
in the mystery, for out in the desert, we have seen
two human shapes moving toward us
too fast to be human. For such beings,
distance is a breath, a word
is not a clay bug, a word is not
your sex pony. Drive me
to the industrial park, watch the brain kick
its little clock against the softening skin. I love it
in your car at night. I love it
in the rain and with the well-worms
in your hair. The two shapes have arrived
even sooner than expected, and they are tapping on your car window
and they aren't twins. *All we understand is force,*
they say, *and we don't*
understand force, either.

THE SCALE OF THE BEAST

REBECCA CHACE

IN THE ARCHIVE LIBRARY at Tufts University a bearded young man opens a cardboard box to show me a relic; about six inches long, wrinkled, gray (too gray, it's been painted) with hairs like iron filings and a metal spike down the middle — it's a little frightening and more than a little obscene. This is the tail of Jumbo the elephant, who died 130 years ago. Circus elephants have always been symbols of gentle majesty, but Jumbo was the first to become a celebrity.

Jumbo was born in Ethiopia, but he died in show business at age 24. It was his fourth season with The Greatest Show on Earth, and he was out for his daily exercise along the train tracks when an unscheduled freight train came around the bend. Jumbo couldn't scramble away fast enough. The cowcatcher at the front of the train was destroyed, the engine derailed, and "The Giant Monarch of His Mighty Race" was killed. Jumbo had once led a herd of 20 elephants across the Brooklyn Bridge to prove to a wary public that the newly constructed bridge was safe. Now he was dead on the tracks in Canada.

By then P. T. Barnum had spent what amounted to a fortune on Jumbo, who was brought over from the London Zoological Gardens in 1882 amidst a storm of publicity — the children had loved riding the elephant at the zoo (even Queen Victoria wanted him to stay) — but a buck is a buck and Jumbo came to New York. A crowd of 10,000, the largest the city had ever seen, turned out for his arrival. His traveling crate was pulled by eight horses and a pair of elephants from the ship's landing in Battery Park to the newly opened Madison Square Garden. (The horses could have done the job — but Barnum had a genius for publicity.) Jumbomania ensued: there were Jumbo mugs, Jumbo playing cards, Jumbo neckties, Jumbo earrings, Jumbo canes; there was Jumbo candy, Jumbo peanut butter, even Jumbo perfume — the "Jumbo" size treats that Americans still guzzle and gobble are our last remnants of the craze. Jumbo had been the star of the three-ring show — though his kingly duties were limited to leading the parade — until his untimely end. At which point Barnum still had a business to run: just because the elephant was dead didn't mean he couldn't go on tour.

Jumbo was not the first circus performer to be displayed after death as long as the public was willing to fork over a nickel. The Mexican "Ape Woman," Julia Pastrana, was mummified for the public by her own showman husband after she died in Moscow in 1860, five days after giving birth to their hirsute son, who lived only three days. The dead infant was presented alongside his mother. (The showman ended up in a Russian mental asylum, where he, too, eventually died. Justice can be cruel in circus stories.)

In Canada in 1885, Barnum knew an opportunity when he saw one — according to his press release, Jumbo had died in the act of saving a baby elephant from an oncoming locomotive. Two days later, Barnum cabled Henry Ward, the most famous taxidermist in the country. The news was making headlines with photographs and drawings of the heroic and violent death of "The Lord of the Beasts," and Barnum wanted Jumbo stuffed before he rotted on the embankment. Ward arrived with his brightest apprentice, Carl Akeley, who had grown up poor on a farm in upstate New York. A loner with a talent for drawing and a fascination for animals, Carl wasn't cut out for the family business. Taxidermy was a common hobby at the time; magazines like *The Youth's Companion* and *The Boone and Crockett Club* gave instructions, and the arsenic powder needed for preservation was easily available at local pharmacies. As a teenager, Carl would spend hours at his taxidermy bench, preparing mounts of small animals and birds. To supplement his new hobby, he also took painting lessons. One relative wrote, "Was he not far more than queer?"

Akeley's older brother had gone to the University of Rochester to escape the farm, but Carl hated school as much as his hometown, and besides, there was no money. When he was hired as a taxidermist at Ward's Natural Science Establishment in Rochester, New York, it was his dream come true; Ward's was the cream of the crop, an exotic charnel house where animals were prepared for display at natural history museums around the country. Its entrance was framed by the jawbones of a whale.

In Canada, Ward and Akeley had to work quickly; the stench from Jumbo's putrefying carcass could have gagged a maggot, Akeley later said. Once salted and packed (six local butchers were hired to help), the elephant's skin alone weighed 1,500 pounds; his bones came to 2,400. Inside Jumbo's stomach hundreds of coins and small toys were found, souvenirs of a life in captivity. Once back in Rochester, Ward received further instructions from Barnum. He wanted *two* Jumbos for display — the mounted skeleton and the taxidermied hide — and here was the kicker: the taxidermied animal should be made to look even larger than the real one.

Akeley was a man of science, not the circus. Eventually he'd develop a new technique to pose dead animals in lifelike positions, but it would be many years before he changed the art of taxidermy forever, and a decade would pass before he was hired to work inside that chateau to Natural History rising up on Central Park West. For now, it was 1885, and this bright young man had his first big assignment, the one that would make his name: to recreate Jumbo the elephant, twice.

He couldn't, however, use Jumbo's bones, and anyway the whole scale of the beast was flimflam. Akeley turned to bent wood and iron to support the hide, and a touch of paint completed the illusion. He then structured the skeleton so that it could travel easily; the skull was detachable and the rib cage and spinal column could be removed and replaced by any roustabout. For three years, Barnum dragged Jumbo around the country, finally donating the beast to Tufts University in 1889, which displayed him as the centerpiece to the "Barnum Museum of Natural History," a building dedicated to science and funded by Barnum, who was a college trustee. Jumbo is still Tuft's mascot, though the carcass itself, monument to Barnum's humbuggery and Akeley's skill, burned in a fire that destroyed the museum in 1975. By then the tail had been yanked off by generations of undergraduates who liked to wag it for luck before their exams. On the morning after the fire, someone from the athletics department gathered up some of the ashes and put them into a Peter Pan Crunchy Peanut Butter jar. That very jar is still brought out to inspire college athletes before a game; but like the shriveled foot of the last Dodo on display in Oxford, England, this tail, tucked away in a white cardboard box in Medford, Massachusetts, is all that remains of "the King of the Elephants."

Carl Akeley never worked for a circus again, but he was nearly killed by an elephant on a hunting expedition for the American Museum of Natural History in what was then called "British East Africa," now Kenya. Akeley's biographer, Penelope Bodry-Sanders, calls this elephant his "white whale." The cover of her book shows Akeley dressed like an aging undergraduate circa 1910 in a three-piece suit complete with watch chain and tie, posed next to a huge elephant skull suspended by a thick rope. He rests a hand near the top of one long, veined tusk as tall as himself. By this time, Akeley had come a long way from Clarendon, New York. He was now recognized as a visionary by the ruling elite, who were developing the American Museum of Natural History in close competition with the Smithsonian Institution in Washington. Six months before he was mauled, in fact, Akeley hunted elephants with President Teddy Roosevelt, who was, himself, on an expedition for the Smithsonian. Like so many great white hunters, Akeley had come to consider himself a conservationist and a scientific collector of specimens.

On this particular morning, he was hunting alone (well, not really alone; he was just the only white man on the scene), unaware that the large male elephant he stalked was apparently similarly interested in him. He'd put down his gun to rub his chilled fingers together when the elephant burst out of the bamboo. With presence of mind that is hard to imagine, Akeley grabbed the tusks and swung himself between them so that he wouldn't be gored. The elephant pressed Akeley to the ground with his forehead and curled trunk, until Akeley heard his ribs crack and passed out. The elephant then pulled away, a tusk ripping Akeley's face apart as the animal stepped back and ran into the jungle. The Kikuyu and Swahili porters scattered, and when they eventually returned they assumed that Akeley was dead. They kept watch over the body so that wild animals wouldn't eat it, and sent a message to Akeley's wife Mickie, back at the base camp, that her husband had been killed. Hours later, Akeley regained consciousness, having been left as a corpse out in the rain. He called for Mickie and whiskey, and when the safari workers realized that he was alive, they brought him closer to the fire. More than 24 hours later, Mickie (Starbuck to his Ahab) arrived and began to clean his wounds as he slipped in and out of consciousness. According to her description, as later told to their mutual friend Roy Chapman Andrews (the real-life model for the film icon Indiana Jones, and author of "Akeley of Africa"),

> Carl was a dreadful sight. The elephant's trunk had scalped his forehead, closed one eye, smashed his nose and torn open one cheek so that it hung down and exposed the teeth in a horrible grin. Many of his ribs were broken. Several had punctured his lung and blood was running out of the corners of his mouth.

It took three days to get Akeley off the mountain and months for him to recover; but after being mauled he was more determined than ever to bring back a large bull of his own.

While he lay in his cot, refusing to leave Africa until he bagged the great male tusker he desired, he conceived of what is now the Akeley Hall of African Mammals almost exactly as seen today at the Natural History Museum.

Months later, in spite of fever, and illness, and hardship, he finally shot an acceptably large bull. At the end of the 1909 expedition Akeley brought four elephants back to the museum, and this time he was able to recreate them as exactly as possible — he even incorporated actual bones from the animals to support the taxidermied hides. The elephant herd took him six years to complete, and in the process he created his new method of taxidermy. It was Akeley the sculptor (a true artist, if inclined to the grisly) who first created a clay model of the elephant, and eventually used a thin layer of clay to reproduce every fold of skin on the actual hide. The clay was then scraped away from the inside and layered with papier-mâché and burlap. The crucial difference this time was that the mold was made to fit the hide from inside out, rather than the hide being stretched over an armature that only approximated — or in Jumbo's case, exaggerated — the animal. Each elephant therefore retained its own specific dimensions and musculature. The animals were no longer ideas of elephants, they had characters as different as they'd had in life. This small invented herd shot by Akeley, Roosevelt's son Kermit, and Mickie (uncredited, the public was told that her elephant was shot by the president, himself) strides through the middle of the African Hall, an eerie sight for tourists when they get lost between the dinosaurs and the butterflies. Children still reach up to stroke their hides.

In the 1980s, Flora, a baby African elephant, was adopted by circus impresario David Balding. Flora had been orphaned by poachers, and at the time, groups concerned about the survival of baby elephants looked for homes for them with circuses and zoos. Flora came to Missouri, and for 20 years she performed in the ring as the namesake of Circus Flora out of St. Louis, well cared for and beloved by her circus family. Balding was practically Flora's father, husband, and brother, but unlike dogs and cats, elephants are more than likely to outlive us. When Balding was in his 60s and Flora was in her early 20s, he knew that it was time to plan for her retirement. As she'd aged, she'd had episodes of unpredictable and violent behavior, perhaps a result of hormonal changes. She no longer belonged in the circus, and he rightly understood that he couldn't take care of her himself. A documentary, *One Lucky Elephant*, was made about Balding's search for the right home, and Flora eventually ended up at an elephant sanctuary in Tennessee, which seemed the perfect solution; the woman who ran the sanctuary had her own performing elephant, now retired. However, once Flora was there, Balding was barred from visiting, and for a time Flora became even more antisocial. Her caretakers clearly believed that Flora had to break her attachment to Balding; to adapt to being a member of a herd rather than continue as a species of human child in an elephant's body. But it was too late — Flora had become a changeling.

It may be easy to say that Flora never should have been adopted, but 30 years ago, this wasn't the way people thought about orphaned elephants. Watching the documentary, it's hard not to empathize with Flora's anger and confusion after she was separated from her human family. Today animal rights activists would probably say that it is better for an orphaned elephant to die in the wild than to become dependent upon human companionship. They'd insist, too (and who could argue?), that it's unnatural for any animal to become a circus performer.

There is a famous Indian parable meant to explain the manifold nature of truth: Six blind men are led into a room with an elephant to learn what the animal looks like. Each of them touches a different part of the body. The man who feels the leg says that an elephant is a pillar. The one who feels the tail says an elephant is a rope. The one who feels the trunk says the elephant is a tree branch. The one who feels the ear says the elephant is a fan. The one who feels the belly says the elephant is a wall. The one who feels the tusk says the elephant is a pipe.

We know that elephants have sophisticated intelligence: they live in matriarchal societies, they are loyal to family members, and they grieve. But it is their eyes, seen close up in so many photographs, that undo us — the dark pupil set into the wrinkled skin can communicate whatever wisdom we decide. This is the gaze that holds us, even when that pupil is made of glass. The dioramas at the American Museum of Natural History almost always have one animal in the group staring out at the humans staring in. This is the impossible moment, held much longer than if one were to actually encounter an animal in the wild. Our own longing to be seen by wild animals is revealed through the way we have captured, killed, and posed them. We force them to look at us longer than they would like.

At the dinner at Ward's Natural Science Establishment following the successful taxidermy of Jumbo, Henry Ward held a banquet for the press. There was a small, colorful booklet published by the circus, describing Ward's great achievement, titled *The Life and Death of Jumbo: An Illustrated History of the Greatest, Gentlest and Most Famous and Heroic Beast That Ever Lived.* Slices of Jumbo's tusk were inscribed for the circus owners with a rampant lion and elephant in the style of the British royal arms above the inscription "Jumbo et mon droit." The crowning dish of the evening was a jelly dessert made with finely ground powder from one of Jumbo's tusks.

Do I believe the whole of the story of Jumbo the elephant? Mostly, yes. I only wonder about the ashes in the peanut butter jar. But this I know for sure: Jumbo's tail is in Medford, and his skeleton is still with the American Museum of Natural History. My repeated requests to see it, evoking the commitment of the museum to the arts, have so far resulted in polite refusals from the Department of Mammalogy. It could be that it is simply too much trouble for the museum to allow a novelist to accompany a conservator to their warehouse in Brooklyn. Or perhaps the museum is uneasy with its complicated colonialist history, and even with the great dioramas that display dead animals for a fee — just as Barnum did in 1866. For the herd of elephants walking through the African Hall is not only evidence of science — it is art and it is theater. The elephants in the Akeley herd are heading toward the front entrance of the museum as if they could pass beneath the skeletons of dinosaurs and march down the steps past the mounted statue of Teddy Roosevelt, flanked by a bare-chested African American and a Native American wearing a ceremonial headdress.

This year, for the first time in its history, Ringling Bros. and Barnum & Bailey Circus announced that it will stop using elephants. They are developing an elephant sanctuary of their own in Florida, where retired performers will still be on view — for a fee.

Although African elephant populations have rebounded slightly from the slaughter that reduced them from some 4 million in the 1930s to 600,000 in the 1980s, they are still being poached and killed at the rate of one elephant about every 20 minutes. Their numbers are on the rise, thanks almost entirely to wildlife preserves managed like enormous, free-range zoos. But it's too late for Flora — David Balding's first choice had been to send her to a sanctuary in Botswana, but when a civil war broke out in the region, he decided that Africa was unsafe. He died in 2014, without ever seeing her again. Flora still lives in the Elephant Sanctuary in Tennessee, but whether or not she misses him, nobody knows.

A friend who worked as a clown in Circus Flora tells me that Flora's trunk once brushed his face during a performance, taking out his contact lens — her touch was so delicate that she left the tiny disc on his eyelashes.

In addition to the books cited, I am indebted to Jumbo: Marvel, Myth, and Mascot *by Andrew McClellan,* African Obsession: The Life and Legacy of Carl Akeley *by Penelope Bodry-Sanders, and* Windows on Nature: The Great Habitat Dioramas of the American Museum of Natural History *by Stephen Christopher Quinn.*

Uncle BEN PACK

"DO YOU WANT MY EGGS?" my sister asked me the day I came out. She wasn't talking about an omelet either. I was shocked. It sounded, well, incestuous. "Not for you," she clarified, her tone suggesting *moron*. "For your future boyfriend — that way you can both be related to your kids."

It's not like I was 14 — like I hadn't considered the idea of having a family. In fact, I had always wanted to be a dad. I came out relatively late (28), and I was still just trying to navigate day-to-day life. My big sister already had two kids, a boy and a girl, and was thinking about a third (18 months later she gave birth to twins). Not that she and her husband are crazy fundamentalists, attempting to be fertile and multiply; they'd just wanted a big family, and she wanted her body back before getting old. "You don't have to make a decision now," she cautioned, "but you should let me know before I'm 35 — eggs don't last forever."

Three years later, living with my boyfriend, when I think about marriage, kids, and our future, part of me goes, yeah, if we have the money and find a surrogate, sure, it would be nice: our children would never grapple with the urge to find their biological parents. Another part of me thinks about that old novelty song "I'm My Own Grandpa." I'd be their dad, but technically their uncle. My sister would be their aunt, but technically their mom — to imagine her egg and my boyfriend's sperm combined in a petri dish, then implanted in someone else's uterus: and who would that woman be? At least adoption is simple to explain — this alternative method requires a chart, and possibly a good family therapist.

Of course these worries say more about my own neuroses than any my kids would develop. I know from watching my sister's children grow from newborns to toddlers — they're their own people, not their genetics. One of the twins prefers adventure (let me climb out of this crib), another caution (let me bury my head in your knee). The eldest, a girl, used to cheep and flap her arms pretending to be a bird; the middle boy got caught peeing in a house plant, because "I'm a dog." So the only thing I can do is keep them from "watering" the ficus, and love them for the creatures they are. Like any good uncle. Like any good brother. That's what my sister was really offering me the day I came out — not only a pipette of pluripotent cells, but also the reassurance that she'd stand by me and mine, whoever I am, whoever we become.

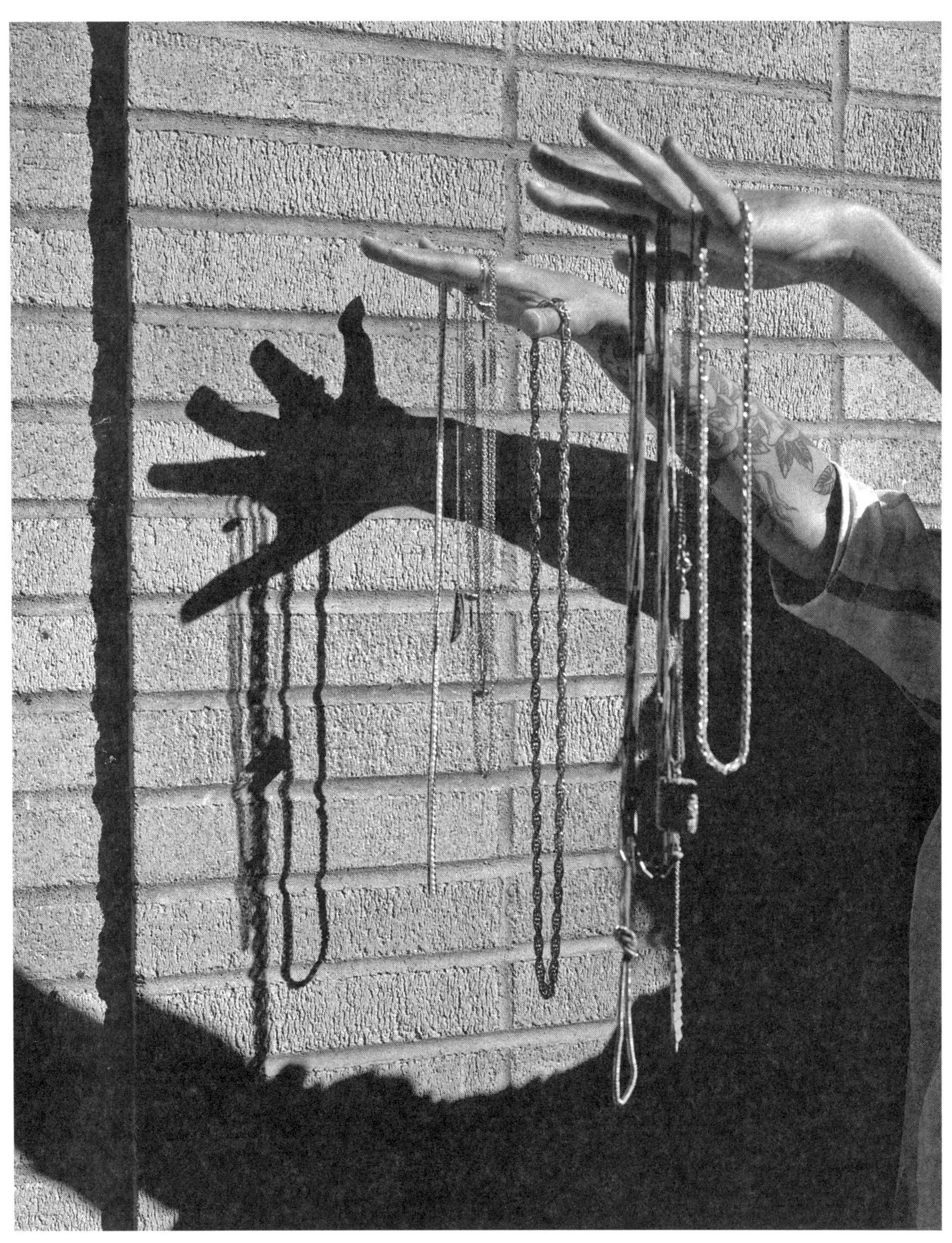

WHITNEY HUBBS
UNTITLED, FROM THE ONGOING SERIES, *MY OWN METAPHORS*, 2015
SILVER GELATIN PRINT, 20 X 16"
COURTESY OF THE ARTIST AND M+B GALLERY, LOS ANGELES

LIFE AFTER ART

PETER GADOL

FOR NO GOOD REASON, my older brother and I had fallen into a habit of not speaking for months at a time, and when we did reach each other, often it was because I initiated an email exchange after spotting him in the fashion pages. I would write something like: *Nice togs.* And Jake would reply: *If you like that sort of thing.* The last time I'd stumbled across him on my way to my morning crossword, Jake was wandering down a Paris runway wearing a white fleece vest, a lime-green bathing suit, and swimming goggles. The *Times* photo ran off-register, and my brother looked like a stunned parrot. I also never knew when he would be coming into the City, and invariably the way I discovered he'd arrived was because a friend texted me while I was at work: *When are we all going to hang out?* Who was we all? *You, me, your brother.* He's here? *You didn't know? Saw him sitting at the café by your building.* And then, predictably: *So hot.*

It was easy enough to picture my brother dressed in a sweater of casually loosening threads, the sleeves too long, sipping a macchiato, gazing at nothing in particular, wondering how on earth he would fill all those morning hours before hitting the gym, and then all those afternoon hours post-gym. *So you guys want to hang out tonight?*

Jake had been in New York for a few days and was ignoring my questions about how long he planned on staying. My model brother could afford a boutique hotel but instead opted for a lumpy sibling couch. When I got home from work, he was stretched out, reading an early chapter of a novel he'd found on my night table. It was one of the last days in October before the radiators would come on, already chilly, and he only had on a pair of cargo shorts.

"Aren't you cold?" I asked.

He was my brother and I loved him, and I would like to say I saw *it*, but I didn't: We were both dark the way our mother had been dark, but only he ended up with her eyes, as cold as a lake. Jake had a way of never seeming in a hurry, neither in speech nor stride. Every doorway became his proscenium. By maintaining a bit of stubble, he'd made excellent money, whereas when I didn't shave, I got stopped at customs.

"Hard day at the office?" he asked, a little glib I thought.

"Yes, actually," I said.

We were in the process of preparing the gallery for a major opening the following week. Our artist had made public that she was very ill, so there was naturally a lot of interest in what would be her final body of work. I did enjoy my assistantship, but what Jake knew (thus his tone) was that this was only a job-job for me until I could start getting my plays produced in a serious way.

"Hungry?" Jake asked.

"Yes, actually," I said again. "How about that posh new Italian place on Tenth?" I knew my brother would pay.

At dinner, Jake decimated a city block of lasagna. I ordered a chicken caesar, no cheese, no croutons, obviously no dressing. I allowed myself one glass of wine, so Jake drank most of the Chianti.

He said, "Let's split the tiramisu."

"You can't still be hungry," I said. "I hate you."

A sudden memory: Jake preparing my afternoon snack, our mother still at school with the math club or the chess club. He would smear peanut butter on a cracker, hand it to me, silently watch me eat the whole thing as if administering medication, and then prepare another cracker. I kept eating the peanut butter crackers as long as he kept handing them to me, like he was training me to break an endurance record.

Jake signaled the waiter. He ordered dessert and a non-nonfat latte, the show-off.

"I'm not big enough," he explained. "Lanky is out. I go home after working out and have a steak and eggs like my trainer says, and nothing. I can't gain a gram."

"Fucker," I said.

The tiramisu arrived, but Jake only pecked at it with his spoon.

"You haven't told me why you're in town," I said. "Do you have a lot of bookings?"

"Look," Jake said. "Can we not talk about that stuff?"

He looked genuinely down about things, so I decided to be a better brother.

"Eat your dessert or you won't get any vegetables," I said, and then I told him about the guy who had dumped me because I'd pointed out a misspelling in his back tattoo. I told my brother about how once and for all I'd parted ways with my theater company because in the process of renaming ourselves, a majority faction had insisted on spelling theater *theatre*. I told him how my boss spilled coffee on a lithograph and rather than fess up to this disaster, she simply changed what was an edition of 12 to an edition of 11. I was making all of this up for Jake's amusement — it worked, he giggled — except for the part about the theater company, not about why I'd quit, but that I had quit. I admitted this.

"When did that happen?" my brother asked.

"A while ago. We've talked since then, haven't we?"

"That was your longest relationship," Jake said.

I hadn't thought of it that way. No, not true, I had.

"So what are you working on?" Jake asked, and I shrugged, and he stared at me, waiting.

"You know I don't like to talk about my writing," I said.

Of Jake's many profitable expressions, frowning wasn't one of them.

"Okay, okay," I said. "So, it's a film about these two men —"

"Not a play? A film?"

"I write screenplays, too," I said.

"I thought you were fairly dedicated to playwriting and the path to poverty."

"Do you want to hear this or not?"

My story was about two young guys, a couple, both struggling artists who are down on their luck. They are sexy, cute together, but one of them is especially pretty. By accident, the prettier guy meets an older man at a church chamber music concert and allows himself to be bought a drink. The pretty guy learns that the older man is dying — and also seeking a companion with whom he can travel around Northern Italy one last time. Key fact: the dying man has no heirs. So the two young guys hatch a plan whereby they will send the pretty one on the Italian sojourn with the dying man with the goal of securing some kind of legacy from him — and then the two young guys will be set for a while, able to pursue their arty life together after the older man dies. However, what couldn't have been anticipated is that, in getting to know the older man, the pretty guy actually falls in love with him; then the dying man dies; and the pretty guy cannot return to his lover with the same passion they knew before because he, the pretty guy, is simply too heartbroken.

Jake blinked at me, unmoved.

"It's a gay *Wings of the Dove*," I explained.

"Oh. I see," Jake said.

"*Oh I see*?"

"No, it sounds neat," Jake said.

"*Neat*. Fine, whatever. Let's not talk about it."

The next morning when I woke up, Jake was making us blueberry pancakes.

"You want me to be fat and lonely the rest of my life, this is your plan," I said, accepting a plate, drenching a stack in syrup.

"I've been thinking," Jake said. "Your plot —"

"I know. *Wings of the Dove* was already pretty queer the first time around."

"No, it's not that. But. I don't know if it's all that filmicky."

"I think you mean cinematic?"

"Sure."

This had occurred to me. I hadn't been able to make it work as a play, or not the kind of play I wanted to sit through. Jake held his fork over his pancakes, and while I could tell he was in a better mood than the night before, he seemed nervous, tentative.

"If you're going to write a film," he said, "maybe you'd like a collaborator? Because it's something I've been thinking about doing. I mean. I can't do *this* forever." Jake waved his hand in a circle around his face.

I was lousy at collaboration. The truth was that I hadn't quit my theater troupe, but rather that they — my college friends — had asked me to leave because I wasn't always so collegial. I had my moods, usually three or four different ones in the space of an hour. I was at a time in my life when I recognized I didn't like myself very much and had resolved to do something about it, but I hadn't yet figured out what exactly.

Jake said, "Remember *Arthur for Arthur's Sake*? I helped you out with that and it turned out pretty well."

This was the one-act play I wrote the summer when I was 14: The son of a famous author plans on murdering his father, who verbally abused him when he was growing up, but instead realizes the harsher punishment would be to torch an unpublished handwritten manuscript. (It was a pre-digital age drama.) He breaks into his father's house one night, holds him at gunpoint, and proceeds to read the manuscript aloud, burning each page as he goes. Except by the time he read-burns most of the novel, he discovers it's a roman à clef about how the author's own father abused him, but much worse than the son was ever tormented by the author. I submitted it to a regional contest and was a finalist; the play was given a reading; I thought I was on my way.

"You proofread it for me," I said.

"Yes — and? I think I made a few suggestions which you incorporated."

Jake was 34; he was at the end of his beauty, and then what would he do with himself? I didn't want to be one more person rejecting him, but I also knew there was no way we could work together.

"I do have one idea I think you'd be into," Jake said.

"This can never work."

"Davey, just think about it. It could be really fun, like old times," he said, and for some reason I thought about the car I backed into at 10 miles an hour when Jake was teaching me to parallel park. We had to wait around for the owner of the car with the cracked front bumper to show up, and Jake kept saying, Don't worry, Davey. We'll laugh about this one day, you'll see.

Sonya Onyva, born 1950, Boston. Currently lives and works in New York. Early success in the mid-1970s largely because she stood out as an artist dedicated to painting when painting wasn't in vogue — large-scale abstract works on canvas at that. Probably because she wasn't a feminist or a conceptualist or an expressionist or even truly an abstractionist (there were, if one read her titles and knew to look, concrete images in her work), she never became an art star. And yet she always had a gallery and earned a living producing 15 to 20 large works every two years along with a steady supply of multiples. Her life was simple: she made art, she sold the art, she made more art. I'd met her the first time at an opening for another one of our artists — this was before her illness — and drunk on white wine, I told her I admired her for the security of her vision and the integrity with which she pursued it. Sonya gripped my arm and drew me closer to clink my glass. She was all silk: Silky long gray-black hair, silky quasi-Japanese flower-print jacket, silky alto whisper: "Vissi d'arte, baby," she said. "Right? Vissi d'arte."

The gallery had already scheduled her show when she called my boss Kristina and revealed her diagnosis: tumors in her stomach, malignant, treatment would only be palliative at best. Kristina was devastated, but she also was determined to give Sonya the last show she deserved and to be shrewd about pre-sales and shore up funds that would provide good college educations for Sonya's nieces. When the work was ready to show, we took clients to Sonya's studio in outer Queens, although Sonya was never around to greet collectors. She insisted her work stand on its own, and of course she wasn't feeling so hot — and without devolving into mawkishness, Kristina italicized the fact that this was the last art Sonya would give the world. Oh, and as the 12 paintings in the show were sold, the price on the remaining work naturally would increase. Nine six-by-eight-foot canvases went for thrice what Sonya had ever received, five of them to museums, and Kristina held back on releasing the final three paintings until the opening.

At one point Kristina said to me, "At least Sonya has lived to see her own revival. Small recompense, but it's something."

I had seen Sonya only once the previous summer and not at all since, and I was apprehensive about accompanying Kristina to Sonya's studio (also I was feeling bloated after eating too many of Jake's pancakes). Sonya had phoned and said she needed to speak with Kristina immediately — it was a conversation that needed to happen in person. I think Kristina was dreading laying eyes on

Sonya as much as I was, which was why I was asked to come along.

However, when the elevator opened onto her cold cement loft, the artist Sonya Onyva, draped in a bright wool shawl, backlit by the morning sun breaking through the grid of factory windows, was the picture of warmth. She looked the way she'd looked when I first met her, hale, self-contained, earth-bound. As we exchanged hugs, I decided that she must have achieved some kind of peace with her immediate destiny (and gratefulness that she'd already lived a good three months longer than initially prognosticated), and now her goal was to make others comfortable with her passage, as well. She handed us mugs of herbal tea. She ushered Kristina off to the back private rooms of the studio and left me with the cloth-gloved art movers, who were delicately positioning the paintings in crates.

Where the canvases had hung on the wall and been worked on, there were now rectangular halos in the nautical palette Sonya had chosen for this series. The studio smelled like linseed oil, like a damp dense forest, like old shoes, like possibility, if possibility had a scent. I studied a canvas propped up against a wall: From copy editing her artist's statement, I knew that Sonya had begun with midcentury photographs taken during deep-sea expeditions, and I didn't have the title of this particular painting handy, but it looked to me like a miniature metropolis of gray-black rock and viridian lichen and silver-crusted who-knew-what, all backdrop to an outgrowth of bloodred coral, coiled and gnarled at its base like a troubled tree, but then opening up, majestic, reaching optimistically toward the surface. I found myself fighting off tears. Only someone very wonderful should own it, I thought.

Kristina and Sonya were hidden away for a half-hour before Kristina alone emerged and hooked my elbow and announced we were leaving. I didn't get a chance to say good-bye to Sonya and almost left with her tea mug in hand. Kristina's eyes were red. Nothing was said until we were in the town car headed back to the gallery. I had to assume that despite appearances the situation was grave. Sonya wouldn't even be able to make it to the opening the following Thursday.

"She's not going to die," Kristina finally said.

"What?"

"I shouldn't be telling you," she said, whispering now, realizing that in New York, our driver could well have connections to whom he could pass along this information.

"But that's good news," I said.

"It's incredible news," Kristina said. "For Sonya. For us, it's more complicated."

As it turned out, one of Sonya's doctors had become suspicious about why she wasn't getting worse and why, in fact, her health in every way seemed to be improving. He returned to old lab results and realized that the lab had, in a mistake that could make Sonya its owner, swapped her results for those belonging to another patient (now deceased). Sonya's tumors were benign. They were problematic, they might well develop into something malicious, but they were not going to kill her.

"I'm ruined," Kristina said.

Ah. I understood the problem. When news of Sonya's misdiagnosis and strong health became known, everyone in the art world and beyond would think that we'd knowingly perpetrated a hoax to drive up the prices of a lesser artist.

"God, I wonder if she knew about this all along," Kristina said.

I was quick to doubt that. It didn't sound like Sonya.

"You're right," Kristina said. "So what do we do?"

"You're asking *me*?"

She was.

I thought aloud: "We shouldn't tell anyone until the show is up. And we can blame it on the doctors, the lab — we do have someone to blame."

"Sonya knows she can probably sue the hospital, but she's rejoicing — she's hardly feeling litigious."

"Her collectors may not feel so generous," I said.

"So we keep it quiet a couple of weeks, but then what?" Kristina asked.

I improvised: "With all of the money she's making, Sonya could disappear and pretend she did die. She could still make art, and we could still show her, but she'd have to go by an alias. The first show by this new artist might need to be an *homage* to Sonya Onyva, because obviously Sonya's style won't evolve that quickly ..."

Kristina squinted at me.

"I'm joking," I said, although I wasn't really.

This was how my mind worked: The story I told myself about where my life (where anyone else's life) was headed always turned out to be a lot more thrilling than the life I eventually led. I would turn 30 in a few months and I wanted to stop obsessing about the future, but all the chatter one heard about living in the present seemed like a lot of bunk to me, impossible to pull off and against my nature.

As we pulled up to the gallery, Kristina said, "I shouldn't have told you, David."

"I can keep a secret," I said.

Kristina held us in the car an extra moment.

"I promise," I said. "Do you want me to get your attorney on the phone?"

All I wanted to talk to my brother about at the bistro that night was Sonya's turnaround, but I kept my word and said nothing. Jake ordered steak béarnaise and a full plate of pommes frites; I had my grilled chicken sauce-less and ixnayed the polenta in favor of sautéed spinach. It was Friday, though, so I was drinking freely.

"Here's my idea," Jake said, wagging a frite at me: A number of people living all around the country, say five or six of them, men and women, young and old, each without any apparent connection to the others, are all struggling in their lives, in marriage or relationships, at work, at school. Each in his or her way has reached a breaking point, and each also finds him or herself compelled for unknown reasons to travel to a distant place, and only once they arrive do they understand that they've all been through a major medical trauma. In fact, all of them have received an organ transplant, and — here was Jake's central concept — they all had received organs from the same donor. Which they somehow figure out.

"It's as if they've been mysteriously assembled because the dead donor isn't at peace," Jake said. "His soul is scattered."

Was this going to be some kind of supernatural horror movie? I could never sit through a horror movie, let alone write one with my brother.

"These people have been drawn together to make Henry whole again," Jake continued.

"Henry is the guy."

"Yes. Henry gave them a second life."

"You need a good setting," I said. "An inn somewhere tranquil, but also where a hurricane could destroy everything."

"I like that, an inn," Jake said, "keeps the cast together. What about Cape May?"

Cape May was where we used to spend the second two weeks of every July with our mother. We never knew our father.

"Good, Cape May, and maybe the inn used to belong to Henry," I said.

"Excellent," Jake said.

"But you're missing the twist. Like maybe it's not simply that Henry isn't whole anymore and therefore unsettled. He's *angry* about it — or rather, his ghost is."

Jake was grinning at me. I'd taken the bait, and he knew it. A plot was a puzzle, and I was addicted to puzzles.

"Why is Henry's ghost so angry?" Jake asked.

I withdrew fries from my brother's plate and thought about it.

"Because his organs were donated against his will," I said.

"I like that," Jake said. "Who is at this inn?"

"A man with the heart, I suppose. Maybe an older woman with Henry's corneas, someone with a lung. The liver, a kidney."

We ordered more wine to keep us fueled. I was compulsively dipping Jake's fries in the béarnaise sauce.

"What if the ultimate reunion is impossible?" Jake asked.

"You mean one of the organs is a no-show? The liver is missing in action?"

This was why the reunion of Henry's body parts was doomed to failure. The film would be stark and bleak. This was more my speed. Although I did have one sudden concern.

"Should we be worried we're giving organ donation a bad name?" I asked.

Jake brushed this off. He said, "So why were Henry's organs donated against his will?"

"His widow wanted revenge because Henry cheated on her," I said as if it were obvious. "And then Henry wants to get back at his widow by becoming whole again and terrorizing her."

"Except the liver doesn't show up," Jake said, "ruining his plan."

"But are we making Henry too much the villain? Shouldn't he be the hero?"

"Maybe Henry's wife was the one who cheated," Jake suggested.

"And Henry caught her in the act, and the wife then responded by murdering Henry in his sleep. And having his organs donated."

"So now the ghost of Henry is seeking revenge," Jake said, "but it's justifiable, we're rooting for him."

"Maybe the cheating wife figures out all of the organ recipients are staying at the inn, and she's the one who locks the liver guy in the attic."

"Okay, but what exactly is put-back-together Henry, assuming he and the other recipients can find the liver guy, going to do that's such a threat to the wife?"

"Well," I said, "he'll go to the police and report who murdered him!"

Jake stared at me: Wait, what? How? And I couldn't claim I understood our story anymore, but I was a little drunk and having fun. This was all merely banter, a silly ridiculous game.

Jake's phone lit up when a message came in, which he made the mistake of reading. He slid the phone back in his pocket and looked glum.

"Monday I have to meet with these catalog people so they can give me the once-over," he said. "I had to set it up myself."

"I take it that's not what you normally do?"

"I can't remember the last time I had to meet anyone first," Jake said. "Catalog people, no less. Do you know why Yvette dumped me?"

I hadn't heard Paris girlfriend's name before. "Because you don't have enough muscle mass?" I asked.

"Don't even joke," Jake said.

I was an idiot. "Why, because she doesn't know you're a classically trained pianist? Because she's never seen you water-ski? Because you read books?"

"She said I was beginning to look my age and didn't seem bothered about it."

"Is Yvette a model, too?"

"Was," Jake said. "She runs my agency's Paris office. My former agency, that is."

I understood better what was going on with him career-wise and offered to pick up half the check, but Jake wouldn't allow it. He was also generous to my friends, buying everyone a round at the gay bar down the street where we ended up next.

My friend, the one who had spotted my brother before I knew Jake was in town, asked him which designers he was modeling for, and Jake said, "Nobody. I'm here writing a screenplay with Davey."

"Oh?" my friend asked. "What's it about?"

And for some reason Jake started to tell him.

"Hey," I interrupted. "You can't go telling everyone our ideas."

"Who am I going to tell?" my friend asked.

"Everyone says that," I said.

The bar was loud, and my older brother had to bend over slightly to shout in my ear: "We need a title. I'm thinking something with Henry in it."

"*Henry Whole*," I said. I was just joking around.

"Too indie," Jake said. "We might be on to something more commercial here."

I pulled back from my brother and studied his face. The blue light in the bar revealed the brackets forming around his mouth, greater-than and less-than signs at his eyes. He was serious, he was dead serious about this whole enterprise, but I was wobbly and a little stoned from a hit I'd taken off a friend's pipe out on the patio.

"Commercial," I said. "Okay. How about *Universal Donor*?"

Jake nodded, good good.

"Or how about just *Donor*," I said.

"Even better," Jake said and kept nodding, until he realized I was making fun of him.

"I'm sorry," I said, trying to recover. "I'm a shitty drunk."

Jake shrugged it off. He mussed up my hair. He checked his watch.

"I need to go somewhere where there are women," he said. "Don't wait up."

"Where's your brother going?" my friend asked.

"I fucked up," I said.

My friend didn't hear me. "Hey, so is he like a total top?"

"He's straight," I said.

"Hot," my friend said, at which point I decided I hated the gays, and I left, too.

Jake came in around three. I tried to be quiet when I got up for work the next morning, but he was awake on the couch. I apologized again for being a jerk at the bar.

Jake released a long sigh. "It's okay," he said. "*Donor* isn't our movie anyway."

"It's not?"

He shook his head no. "No. Too schlocky. Not us. Not what we're about."

I wanted to ask him what in fact we *were* about, but I didn't. I squeezed his knee beneath his blanket.

"We'll come up with something else," I said, although Jake looked doubtful, as if every man had one bright idea in him, and his was now mud.

The dejected teenage son of an aging rock star returns to Los Angeles after he's involved in an accident back East at his boarding school — someone in the car he was driving was killed. The son learns his father has phase-four lung cancer, but the rock star is inspirationally upbeat: "I've been dying my whole life," he says. "A rock star is always dying." The dying rock star and his son take a road trip somewhere.

Alibi, Incorporated: A Japanese company creates false cover-up trails for unfaithful husbands, going so far as to establish misleading cell phone records and credit card expenditures for meals never eaten and trips never taken. All goes well until the company's clients begin to disappear from their actual lives and the false stories the company has created become reality. One client dies, and then things really get out of hand. "Lying / is an art, like everything else. / I do it exceptionally well," wrote Sylvia Plath. "I do it so it feels like hell."

A jaded female assistant district attorney discovers her key witness has invented her testimony, and this ADA has 24 hours to go around an urban neighborhood rounding up new witnesses who will help make her case against a truly heinous serial rapist-murderer. The story takes place in one day, and everything that can go wrong does (her car breaks down, she loses her phone, she's nearly mugged, etc.). Who must she rely on to find a new witness and in the meanwhile save her own soul?

"The first one sounds like a young adult novel," Jake said. "Not that that's bad, but I don't know about it as a movie."

He was walking me first to a coffee shop and then to the gallery. I was reading from the pocket journal in which I scribbled the odd thought.

"It originally was going to be a YA novel," I confessed.

"And I think I've seen the second one," Jake said.

Ouch. But I had to admit he was probably right.

"And the third idea — we've seen that, too, haven't we?"

"Have we?" I asked.

"Everything has already been on television now," Jake said. "That's the problem. Also, by the way, Plath wrote, '*Dying* is an art.' Not *lying*."

"She did?"

"I'm the one who gave you *Ariel*," Jake said.

He'd come home from college one holiday break and I'd like the look of the slim white collection with outlined black letters. Jake was eying a harmonica I'd bought and which I couldn't figure out how to get any notes out of. He traded the book for the harmonica, although I don't know that he ever figured out how to play it either. It was easy to forget that once upon a time he'd wanted to become a writer, too. We walked several blocks in silence. I wasn't too keen on the fact that he'd shot a single mortal arrow through each of my meager ideas, and now he was (albeit accurately) correcting my citations.

"Have you noticed that everything we come up with involves death?" Jake asked.

"Enough with the penetrating observations," I said.

Kristina was out on the sidewalk in front of the gallery, checking the window stencil treatment: *Sonya Onyva: Deep Waters.*

"You're David's brother Jake," she said in a kindergarten-teacher voice, as if Jake might have forgotten he was related to me. "We've met before. You're coming to our opening, I hope?"

Before Jake could answer, Kristina said to me, as if this were my first task of the day, "Make sure your brother is at the opening."

But look at him, I wanted to say, he's too lanky, and lanky is out. Let me find some more manly men for you, if you want me to dress the set with models.

"We'll think of something," I said to my brother in parting. "I have plenty more ideas where those came from."

"Sure, Davey," Jake said. It made me sad when he didn't believe me — or rather, when he knew I was lying (not an art apparently I was so good at).

Sonya's paintings had arrived and sat in their crates around the gallery roughly where they would hang. The full staff was on hand and we had a lot of work to do, but Kristina invited me into her office and shut the door. A plan was in place: she would "learn" the truth about Sonya after the opening.

"But we already know," I said.

"No, we don't," Kristina said. "I don't, and you certainly don't."

"I see."

At Kristina's suggestion, Sonya had agreed to put the account of her misdiagnosis in writing and submit it to the gallery in two weeks. (This approach came from Kristina's lawyer, who couldn't technically know about any sort of collusion to circumvent fraud, but who could confidentially advise Kristina about hypotheticals.) Sonya was so grateful she wasn't ill, she was willing to cooperate; and then also she was likely going to end up with some kind of payment from the hospital anyway (she said a lawsuit was inevitable now; she, too, had sought counsel). Kristina would then walk the moral high ground and pass along the "news" to everyone who'd paid the steep price for Sonya's not-so-final paintings, and they would have the option of returning the work or of getting a rebate maybe; or they might choose to accept that in overpaying they'd added worth to work they now held which might, who could predict, hold that value when Sonya did one day die for real. Think of the press she'd get when she made her good health known, and of the critical acclaim she might receive for work made with the honest belief it was valedictory. All to say, a collector might want to hang on to a *Deep Waters* painting because it might one day prove to have been a shrewd investment. Also it was possible the collector genuinely admired and enjoyed possessing the painting quite apart from the recent biography of the painter. The art did have a life of its own, didn't it?

"So the thing is, David, for this to work," Kristina said, "I will officially tell you about Sonya with a bunch of other people in the room, probably next week, week after that at the latest. Until then …"

I heard Kristina's instructions, but then I wasn't really listening because I was staring at a postcard we'd made for the show, another abstract landscape, 90 percent ocean, happier shallower blues pushing back in vain against a rising tide of darker violent greens. There was the hint of a coast, mountains. No sky, of course, never any sky. Only the truly dying needed sky.

Sunday Jake and I sat around my apartment in our pajamas and came up with nothing. Monday evening, we played three consecutive Scrabble games to avoid real conversation. By Tuesday night, Jake was convinced we were tapped out, and he was in about as grim a mood as I'd ever seen him: the meeting with the catalog people had gone particularly poorly.

"I met a girl though on the way out," he said.

"Well, see? You've still clearly got some game left. Will you call her?"

"Doubtful," Jake said.

He was my older brother, and he'd always looked out for me. All I wanted was to cheer him up. I knew what I was about to do was a mistake, but I couldn't help myself.

And so I said, "An artist receives a bad diagnosis, brain cancer, he will be dead in three months. He's not old, he was in many ways at his peak. Resigned now, accepting his destiny, he paints his last paintings — and they're amazing, simply brilliant and amazing. His gallery begins selling them while they're still hanging on his studio wall, and they sell for crazy prices because he's dying. *But …*"

Jake pulled himself up on the couch: Yes, but what?

"It turns out the artist isn't dying! He was misdiagnosed! But here he's sold all of this art for a fortune and achieved fame he's never previously known — what's he going to do now?"

"It's a comedy," Jake said.

"It's a comedy, but there's tragedy right beneath the surface."

"I like it," Jake said. "I like it a lot."

He pushed himself off of the couch and stepped over to the armchair where I was sitting with my knees pulled up to my chest. He hugged me, knees and all.

"There's a lot to work out," I said. "We don't know where it goes or how it will end."

"I really like it," Jake said. I'd made him grin again.

"But don't talk to anyone about it," I said. "Promise me you won't tell anyone."

"I promise," he said. And then: "We need to think about a love interest. That's going to be crucial, don't you think?"

Over the next two days, I put in long hours at the gallery and didn't overlap in the apartment too often with Jake, but clearly he was fired up, as evidenced in the notes he left for me under refrigerator magnets:

What if the artist really needs the money for something (like a depressed wife and-or mentally disturbed child depending on him), so he can't give it back when he finds out he's not dying?

How about the artist falls in love with a gallery assistant but has to pretend he's dying? Would she be attracted to him if he were well (which after all, he is)? Does he have to keep pretending to be sick so she'll love him?

Maybe to avoid accusations of fraud, he pretends to die (even the gallery folks think he's dead), and he takes all the money and starts life over with a new name. But he can't stop painting, and so he signs new paintings with a new name and tricks the old gallery into taking him on and giving him a show. But he can't come to the show — so he sends someone else to pretend to be him? What happens when he's found out?

I had to admit that this last note, scrawled around the margins of a magazine subscription card, made me wonder if certain stories were genetically embedded in us. Were we destined to think the same thoughts? In any case, it was pleasant to hear Jake whistling again. Another thing he'd taught me to do, whistle, and which he could do much better than I ever could.

The thought that Sonya might fake her death and start over became so real to me that I very nearly asked her at her opening if she'd already picked out an alias. Everyone including me was dutifully clad in black jackets and black jeans and black boots, but Sonya had come dressed in a long white dress. Her left arm was sheathed in silver bangle bracelets, which collected like a slinky at her elbow whenever she brushed her hair back from her face. She was the radiant goddess of second chances, but of course no one but me (and Kristina) saw it. The opposite: Sonya's devotees patiently took turns approaching her, taking both her hands in theirs, swinging her arms a little as if to say, See, you still got a little life left in you, old gal.

I heard someone say, "We'll get through this — we will, we will."

And someone else: "You're leaving us all of this tremendous art. We will always have your art."

Sonya faked graciousness so convincingly that I wondered if Kristina's flickering question in the town car back to Manhattan had been more on the money than I'd thought: Maybe this whole scheme was the greatest work of an artist past her prime; she'd forged her illness; we were, all of us, duped. But honestly I didn't want to pass through life as the suspicious sort, and I decided she'd been honest all along.

I was standing near Sonya in the middle of the gallery when Jake arrived. I hadn't seen him since early that morning and assumed he'd forgotten about the opening since it hadn't come up since Katrina's in-passing invitation. However, there he was in inky jeans and a crisp half-unbuttoned shirt, in cowboy boots, his open blazer flapping back against a breeze that appeared to reach only him.

"Hey, Davey," he said.

"You're here."

"Of course I'm here. I'm Jake," Jake said to Sonya Onyva.

"My older brother," I explained. "By five years," I added for some reason.

"I see the resemblance," Sonya said.

"I doubt that," I said.

Kristina had sashayed into our circle and hooked Jake's arm, claiming him.

"The paintings are wonderful," Jake said, and Sonya thanked him. "Large," he said. "And very blue."

We chitchatted for a bit, and then Kristina said she had someone she wanted Jake to meet (why would she want him to meet anyone?), and meanwhile I had to step aside so more adorers could queue up to offer Sonya their condolence-congratulations. Kristina ushered Jake over to an older woman, a collector whose shiny choker and earrings looked like dentist's tools. The collector stood very close to Jake when she spoke with him, and I could see that if my brother wasn't careful, in a few years he'd become a kept man: His days would look very much like they looked now, all about fitness and nutrition and skin care, but on the side he would be *studying* photography, and in the evenings he would rely on intermission espresso to stay awake at the opera.

When I joined the conversation, my brother immediately said to me, flatly, "Natalie here was just telling me about Sonya's illness. I had no idea. How sad."

Kristina placed one hand over her heart. "It's tragic is what it is," she said.

"We must be grateful she's been able to give us these final paintings," Natalie the collector said.

"Grateful," Kristina echoed. She pivoted toward Jake: "If you knew you were dying, what more would you give the world with what time you had left?"

Natalie hummed — what a good question — and she herself was likely trying to come up with some outsized philanthropic act.

"I don't know," Jake said. "I'm not sure I've given the world anything yet."

This answer struck me as deeply troubling, especially when I had to consider my own paltry legacy of scripts, a handful of which had been staged over three consecutive weekends and forgotten.

"You're still young," Kristina said.

"But what if I wasn't really dying," Jake said, staring straight at me. "I mean, I thought I was, but I then I wasn't — what would I do then?"

Kristina now glared at me, as well.

"Maybe I was misdiagnosed," Jake said, "but I'd said my good-bye's. Would everyone I knew be disappointed by my sudden health?"

Natalie gripped her silver choker in dismay, and Kristina said, "Jake, in this context, with what Sonya's going through, that's not a very appropriate comment."

"I'm sorry," Jake said. This was unlike him. He was the last person on earth to make trouble.

Kristina escorted Natalie to an adjacent group of Sonya admirers, leaving me alone with my brother.

"What the fuck are you doing?" I asked. I didn't bother pretending like he was misguided with whatever assumptions he was pursuing.

"What am I doing? What are *you* doing?" he asked back.

Kristina rejoined us. To Jake, she said, "I don't know what you know, but whatever you know is wrong." And to me: "You're fired."

"Kristina," I said.

"Effective immediately. Leave. Right now, please," Kristina said. "If you say anything, I swear I'll come after you. Never set foot in here again."

"Kristina," I said again, although it was useless.

"Out," she said. "Both of you, now." And with that she returned to hostess mode and double-kissed two men in identical gray suits.

Out on the sidewalk in front of the gallery, Jake said, "Is it true? She was dying, but now she's not?"

"It's a good story," I said, my only defense.

"It's somebody else's story," Jake said, "which you apparently stole."

"Art is based on real life all the time," I said.

"But you didn't tell me that. I thought you came up with it on your own. I was proud of you."

That hurt. I didn't react well. I started walking away from the gallery, Jake behind me, and it was sinking in that Kristina wasn't joking, and I had no job and therefore no way to pay the November rent. I swung back around and faced my brother:

"Where do you think ideas come from, Jake? You make the most of what's in front of you. Isn't that what we do? Isn't that how we get by? Not that you would know about getting by, not that you've ever had to do more than take off your shirt and not blink and look like you have real thoughts in your head. You might have to do a shoot for a clothing catalog, and it's like the world is ending. Hey, there are other people out there with much bigger problems."

What was wrong with me? When had I become so mean?

Jake's shoulders sloped down. "Of course there are," he said.

We stood there a moment, and then Jake said something about seeing me back at my apartment, turned, and headed around the corner and was gone. The one thing I could say I safely possessed was his respect, and now I didn't have that. But I had wanted him to be happy (which he was for two days), didn't he see that? Or was that even really true? What I'd wanted was to show off. What I'd wanted was to renew his belief in me.

I couldn't go home yet, so I ended up at a bar talking to a guy who taught geography and history to seventh graders. He was cute and fit and smart, more datable than anybody I'd met in a long while, but I couldn't focus and lost track of what he was telling me — something about how he wanted combat pay for working with adolescents, something about how he'd suffered through a parent conference that afternoon and his student's mother was worse than the kid, checking texts during the meeting —

I latched on to the word mother. I remembered the date. I apologized, asked for the guy's number, and said I needed to leave. I headed for my corner grocery, but they didn't have what I needed and I settled for a pack of vanilla-scented tea candles, which would have to suffice.

My apartment was dark, and at first I didn't think Jake had come home yet. Then my eyes adjusted to the candlelight: He was sitting on the couch, arms crossed, legs crossed, still in his gallery-going outfit, minus the jacket and boots. The candle he'd picked up was the right kind of candle. Its flame was thin and fragile and gave off meager light.

"I only remembered walking back. Nine years," Jake said. "Where did nine years go?"

When he bought the yahrzeit candle, he'd also picked up some mint chocolate chip ice cream, my favorite. I think he emptied the whole pint into two bowls, and when he handed me mine, I said, "Hi."

"Hi," Jake said.

"I'm sorry," I said.

"Whatever."

"No, not whatever. I'm really, really sorry," I said, and that could have been that.

However, Jake said, "I got excited. Nothing else has excited me lately."

"I know," I said. "And I let you down."

"You didn't let me down, Davey. But from here on out, why don't you let me be the sellout?"

I didn't know what to do with this comment. I needed to turn it over, it wasn't true. His modeling career was accidental. It was a fun way to move through his 20s and early 30s, and he'd made crazy money, he'd traveled everywhere — why not? It was temporary. Now he could do other things with his life.

"Please," I said, "you're hardly a sellout —"

"Mom wouldn't like our movie, if we made a movie," Jake said.

"I disagree."

"She didn't like movies for some reason. I don't know why."

"But she always was reading three books at a time," I said.

Jake chuckled. "Do you remember how she would read the endings first?"

"That drove me nuts. How could she do that?"

"She said then she could enjoy the book because she wasn't anxious about how things would turn out."

My brother was the only being on earth who remembered me when I was young. What had I been like as a child? If ever I forgot, he could tell me.

"There was the phase when you were into maps and wanted to be a cartographer," Jake said. "And there was the time you wanted to be a rabbi."

"I wanted to be a rabbi because I liked the leather-bound books in the rabbi's office."

"And then I think you were going to be a research scientist."

"Genetics."

"It was always something," Jake said. "A Senator, a playwright."

"Mom humored me."

"She said you could be anything," my brother said.

"You, too," I said.

"Maybe. Especially you though," he said.

We were staring at the yahrzeit candle as if we expected it to do something, surprise us in some way. The surprise was that it would burn for 24 hours, this little juice glass of milky wax.

"You're not a sellout," I said. "When you think about it, you've actually accomplished quite a lot —"

"Be quiet, David," my brother said. "Davey," he corrected himself. "Seriously. You could be anything."

WHITNEY HUBBS
UNTITLED, FROM THE ONGOING SERIES, *MY OWN METAPHORS*, 2015
SILVER GELATIN PRINT, 16 X 20"
COURTESY OF THE ARTIST AND M+B GALLERY, LOS ANGELES

Therapy IRA SUKRUNGRUANG

WE ARE HERE, on this seedy side of this city, waiting to see our lovely daughter who tried to take her life.

We are here, this parental unit, stripped bare and raw from hours in the emergency room nights ago, watching our daughter cry and shudder and say she sees people *so many people* and colors, *so many colors*.

We were there, then, waiting and watching and worrying, through the Poison Control's mandatory 24-hour monitoring period, in a pediatric ICU with elephants on walls, tails and trunks linked, walking toward the only window of the room that overlooked a concrete parking garage.

We were there when two days later Transport took our daughter, our lovely daughter, to a psych ward for an evaluation, on this seedy side of the city where we find ourselves now, where on arrival she heard the cry of a husky seven-year-old boy, who didn't *want want want* to be here, who only *wants wants wants* to go home, who *hates hates hates* everything about this place.

We are here now, during the visiting hour, 6-7 pm, the two of us in this cramped lobby with other parents waiting to see their own lovely daughters or sons, and it is chaotic the way crazy houses are chaotic: a teenaged mother tries to still a bawling baby with a pacifier; the outside intercom's electric buzz echoes through the brown wallpapered room, more parents demanding to be let in; the ins and outs of other sons and daughters, some strapped down on gurneys, some in hospital gowns that flare open in the back; one of those daughters doesn't care, her eyes heavy and lost, as her mother sighs and tries to hold the gown together; and there is the constant reminder from tough-as-hell counselors of no phones or keys, no strings or sharp objects, no more than two people visiting at a time and if you upset the patient you leave; a toddler with deep dimples runs and screeches in and out of a therapy room, utterly joyous, as her older sister in facility green sweatpants chases after her and blows on her tummy, and there is a happiness that happens with this family, no matter how brief, happiness in the face of this toddler, who knows nothing beyond her current contentment, happiness that is like the welcome of sun after months of clouds.

We are here, and we think, we are not these people; we do not have a disturbed child; we do not have a daughter or son who screams and hits and calls us names; we are better than these people, better parents, except our daughter, our lovely daughter, took sleeping/thyroid/muscle relaxing pills, except she hurt, except she suffered silently despite us being there, always there, which makes us feel powerless, helpless, useless.

We are here because we are no different from them; we are them.

And when the therapist opens the door to the visiting room of white concrete and cafeteria tables, she is there, picking at her chipped black-painted nails, the green of a bad dye job bleeding out of her brown head of hair; she is there, our lovely daughter, waiting for us, and when she raises her eyes and sees we are here, she smiles, and how that buckles our knees, how that takes our breath away.

We are here.

"THIS BARREN LAND"
BOB DYLAN'S GOSPEL VARIATIONS

MAX NELSON

SOME 70 YEARS before Bob Dylan recorded *Time Out of Mind*, the album that gave his career the most recent of its many jump-starts and reinventions, the Memphis street-corner gospel singer Blind Mamie Forehand and her husband — a guitar player identified only as "A.C." — laid down a chilling, funereal 78 that quickly found its way into the gospel-blues canon. The legendary Virginian country trio The Carter Family recorded versions of both sides in the 1930s; several decades later, an all-female a capella gospel troupe would take its name from the famous A-track's refrain. The song in question, "Honey in the Rock," is the kind of spectral, imposingly vulnerable performance at which certain prewar Southern gospel singers — Washington Phillips, Blind Willie Johnson, and Homer Quincy Smith, among others — were especially skilled: an eerie invocation backed by a quavering guitar and the regular chiming of a tiny bell.

Forehand's voice on the record's B-side, "Wouldn't Mind Dying If Dying Was All," is firmer and more assertive than on "Honey in the Rock." As the guitar trudges along behind her, she utters what might be a confession and what is certainly — whatever else it is — a warning:

After death, you're gonna have to stand a test
After death, you're gonna have to stand a test
After death, you're gonna have to stand a test
I wouldn't mind dying if dying was all

One of the most striking and elusive aspects of Dylan's recent music — particularly the loose triptych of *Time Out of Mind*, *Modern Times*, and *Tempest* — is the way it channels the tone of American gospel songs like these. The voice that dominates songs like "Love Sick," "Standing in the Doorway," "Trying to Get to Heaven," and many of the numbers on Dylan's subsequent records was a half-secularized variation of the one that still emanates from that couple's only 78: a voice that takes life for something tenuous, fragile, and short, that shuffles around on shadowy thresholds, that lives in a state of constant homelessness, that wouldn't mind dying if it could only be *sure* that dying was all.

1

Since the release of *Time Out of Mind*, Dylan has never stopped accruing myths and rumors, making feints, leaving false trails. He wanders vagrant-like into Long Branch, New Jersey, inquiring about buying Bruce Springsteen's old house. A self-trained boxer, he enters the ring with Ray "Boom Boom" Mancini and asks him, after some light sparring, to "take it a little easy on the head." He releases a critically lauded collection of original songs between an album of Great American Songbook covers and a Christmas record featuring, among other standards, a Latin rendition of "O' Come All Ye Faithful (Adeste Fideles)" and a shiver-inducing, menace-soaked "Little Drummer Boy."

His recent self-effacing insistence, during a rambling, caustic, and startling speech at the Los Angeles Convention Center, that anyone could have written "Blowin' in the Wind" who had sang "John Henry" as often as he had — "I just opened up a different door in a different kind of way" — was no new revelation. It's well known that Dylan's songwriting process has always been a matter of embellishing or reshuffling folk standards. Nor was it a new admission from Dylan himself, who once described (in his autobiography *Chronicles, Volume One*) having honed his skills as a young songwriter by "slightly altering" one melody over and over to produce new songs, once in a while "slipping in verses and lines from old spirituals or blues." But it was an invitation for critics to undertake the same sort of exercise on Dylan's later work that Greil Marcus and others performed on records like *The Basement Tapes* and *Blonde on Blonde*: a slapdash inventory of the ways in which certain strains of early American music found their way into the tone, texture, and mood of Dylan's songs. In the case of these more recent records, it's early American religious music that took a particular hold on Dylan's imagination.

Starting with *Time Out of Mind*, you could argue, Dylan made a sustained effort to capture the peculiar morbid tone of the old spirituals: their obsession with fretting over, guessing, or confidently asserting what comes after death. At the start of what would become one of his most celebrated songs, Washington Phillips asked himself what "they" were "doing in Heaven today." He gave himself a quick answer: "I don't know, boys, but it's my business to stay here and sing about it."

It was indeed a business: the singers and preachers who made a living recording gospel music in the 1920s and '30s very often did so on the strength of their ability to evoke what life would look like in the world to come, for the saved as well as the damned. The Rev. A.W. Nix's sermon "The Black Diamond Express to Hell" was popular enough to inspire five follow-up recordings. Before his imprisonment at Parchman Farm, Delta blues singer and guitarist Washington "Bukka" White had a successful stint at Victor Records in the early 1930s recording optimistic spirituals like "The Promise True and Grand" and "I Am in the Heavenly Way." Some of the most powerful early gospel recordings, like those featuring Bessie Johnson, a formidable singer whose earth-shaking voice was a fixture of the Memphis Church of God in Christ for years, pivoted on promises of redemption ("One Day"; "He Got Better Things for You"; "Since I Laid My Burden Down") or doom ("The Great Reaping Day," Rev. Johnny Blakey's "Warming by the Devil's Fire"). At his last recording session (the Depression put an early end to his career), the hugely popular preacher F.W. McGee cut a boisterous, vividly detailed picture of what "better things," exactly, the Lord had in store for His people. Harry Smith included the recording on his legendary *Anthology of American Folk Music*, and Dylan, one imagines, readily soaked up the tone of the song's chorus:

> When the gates swing wide on the other side
> Just beyond the sunset sea
> There'll be room to spare as we enter there
> Room for you and room for me
>
> For the gates are wide on the other side
> Where the flowers ever bloom
> On the right hand, on the left hand
> Fifty miles of elbow room.

The lyrics are confident, prophetic. There *will* be room to spare on the other side, where the gates *are* wide, provided you have passed the test that — an implicit spiritual echo of Blind Mamie Forehand — you're *gonna* have to stand. Assurance, however, is rarely the dominant tone in this strain of prewar gospel, which lends itself more often to doubt and discomfiture. Often, the doubt comes out in the music itself, in the texture of the singer's voice and the restless, clattering, spectral movements of the backing instruments. Listen past the swaggering bluster of Brother Claude Ely's 1953 recording of "There Ain't No Grave (Gonna Hold My Body Down)," which the preacher allegedly wrote in divine inspiration during a childhood bout with consumption, and you'll hear a fidgety, anxious tone to match its occasional, abashed conditionals ("If these wings should fail me / Want you to meet me with another pair") and implorations ("Gabriel don't you blow your trumpet / Until you hear from me"). Dylan's late music is more agnostic, more openly skeptical than any of these prewar gospel numbers, but the morbid doubt that surfaces on records like *Time Out of Mind* and *Modern Times* was already written into early gospel music's genes.

Oddly, when Dylan underwent a high-profile conversion in the early 1980s, the gospel records he started making were of a decidedly modern, postwar breed: roof-shaking, lavishly produced, choir-backed songs of perseverance and praise. Some of this music, particularly the magisterial *Shot of Love*, has aged well; much of it less so. The reassurance that fills "Death Is Not the End," a schmaltzy, ballad-like spiritual that appeared midway through 1988's *Down in the Groove*, is the stuff of condolence note boilerplate: "When the storm clouds gather 'round you / And heavy rains descend / Just remember that death is not the end."

It was with the pair of albums he made between 1992 and 1993 — *Good as I Been to You* and *World Gone Wrong* — that Dylan found his way back to earlier, prewar strands of folk and blues, and it was on *Time Out of Mind* and its follow-ups that he rediscovered the spirit of early American spirituals. Like generations of listeners before him, Dylan saw through the promises and threats those songs proffered up front. What he'd come upon instead were deep reserves of doubt, anxiety, rootlessness, and pain.

2

Exhausted, burnt-out, and heavy-limbed, many of the songs on *Time Out of Mind* and *Modern Times* suggest the fear of a pilgrim unsure of reaching — or having — a destination. The narrator of "Love Sick," the first song on *Time Out of Mind*, makes his entrance "walking through streets that are dead"; that of "Standing in the Doorway" is introduced "walking through the summer nights"; that of *Modern Times*'s "Ain't Talkin'" is, he insists, "just walkin' / Through this weary world of woe." (Similar images appear throughout *Time Out of Mind*'s centerpiece "Not Dark Yet" and its wry outtake "Marchin' to the City.")

Listen to any number of songs by the influential sacred country duo The Blue Sky Boys, who made their first recordings in Charlotte, North Carolina, near the end of 1936, and you'll hear the same fear assigned a litany of causes. But in recordings like "Only Let Me Walk with Thee," the B-side of the plaintively titled "No One to Welcome Me Home," there's no cause for fear named but the vague work of "toiling on life's pilgrim pathway" — the uncertainty of walking when "the way is hedged in darkness / And the path I cannot see." For another tonal spin on the pilgrim song, it's revealing to pass over the strict color line record labels invariably drew between "race records" and "hillbilly records" in the years before World War II. Many of the African-American vocal groups that came to prominence in the '20s and '30s — The Golden Gate Quartet; South Carolina Quartet; Mound City Jubilee Quartette — developed a distinctly less fragile, more muscular variation on the form. Sung by black male singers under the thumb of an exploitative and racially prejudiced recording industry in the prewar South, lines like "I'm a pilgrim and a stranger / Traveling through this barren land" lose some of their vague forlornness and take on a more lacerating power.

It's to the *city* that the characters in most of Dylan's pilgrim narratives are marching, and into the specific sort of loneliness that word evokes. The singers might be trapped in a grid-like network of streets, like the characters who narrate "Love Sick," "Standing in the Doorway" ("I got no place left to turn"), and an unreleased demo recorded in 2005 for *Modern Times* ("I don't like the city / Not like some folks do / Isn't it a pity / I can't escape from you"), but the songs themselves are capacious, slippery, and porous, full of unexpected resonances, elongated syllables, and generous stretches of space in which notes can be cushioned and absorbed.

Who are the narrators on *Time Out of Mind*? Where are they going? Are they on the run? ("Maybe they'll get me and maybe they won't," the speaker of "Standing in the Doorway" mumbles as if to himself, "But not tonight and it won't be here.") Their ways are hedged in darkness, but they take their relegation to those ways as an occasion for doubt, resentment, ambivalence, and silence. For them, words have worn out their use; often, as in "Standing in the Doorway," they run down the clock on their songs by verbally confessing — or testifying to — their need to give up speech: "I see nothing to be gained by any explanation / There are no words that need to be said."

Those lines emerge from Dylan's body cracked, dusty, and dried out. On *Time Out of Mind* his voice has none of the enveloping roundness of certain early gospel singers (a tone that — as shown on the magisterial rendition of "That Lucky Old Sun," which closes his most recent record, *Shadows in the Night* — he's more than capable of), or any of the tremulous vulnerability, confident swagger, or meek submissiveness of others. It's a rasp, a whine, a bruised and bruising energetic force. Like the drifters and highwaymen it's been shaped to resemble, it can do damage by virtue of having been out walking too long.

3

It can also pine. If songs like “Standing in the Doorway” or “Love Sick” are corrupted pilgrim narratives, they often equally resemble warped, dispirited love songs. On *Modern Times*, Dylan’s second record after *Time Out of Mind* (it was preceded by the sweeping *Love and Theft*), we’ve been returned to a moment in the history of songwriting before the sacred and the secular were exclusive arrangements, when the same performers could move with ease between spirituals, folk legends, disaster songs, and brokenhearted blues laments. Now, however, the range of possible combinations has widened to include, among other ingredients, Vegas-style lounge singing (“Spirit on the Water”), accordion-driven Southwestern waltzes (“This Dream of You” from *Together Through Life*) and flickering cowboy laments (“Nettie Moore”).

In the canon of prewar American folk music, it’s hard to find a secular singer who never recorded sacred numbers. Bluesmen like Charley Patton, Henry Thomas, and Bukka White achieved some of their most indelible, haunting effects on spirituals. (What might be Patton’s finest recorded song — “Some of These Days I’ll Be Gone” — is, revealingly, neither a spiritual nor a blues number, but an imaginative revision of a Tin Pan Alley hit by Sophie Tucker, although the scholar Richard Middleton is right, I think, to call the result “hymnlike.”) One of the greatest of all prewar gospel songs, Kid Prince Moore’s “Church Bells” was the work of a musician otherwise best known for singing lines like “If that’s your woman, pin her to your side / ’Cause if she flag my train I’m sure gonna let her ride.” The stigma attached to such racy numbers in certain churches at the time kept a subset of gospel singers from broadening their repertoires, but it didn’t stop the sauciness, insouciance, and sexual energy of secular folk and blues from bleeding into the country’s sacred music.

There was always a particularly close correspondence between romantic and spiritual longing in early American recorded music: both were matters of wandering, of loneliness, of redemption promised and deferred. One of Dylan’s signature moves on *Modern Times* is to yoke both sorts of longing together in the space of a single song. “Spirit on the Water” begins with an invocation of the Bible passage from which it takes its title (“Darkness on the face of the deep”) before veering into a markedly different tone: “I keep thinking ’bout you, baby / and I can’t hardly sleep.” It’s a pilgrim song that pivots on mischievous substitutions, falling into a tender romantic groove just when it seems best primed to abandon such worldly matters:

> I’ve been trampling through mud
> Praying to the powers above
> I’m sweating blood
> You got a face that begs for love

The promise that runs through “Nettie Moore” and “Spirit on the Water” is of a kind of romantic consolation — the kind the songs’ narrators can only attain after, as the singer of “Nettie Moore” puts it, everything they’ve “ever known to be right has been proven wrong.” Requesting that sort of consolation involves careening from threats (“Before you call me any dirty names, you better think twice”) to boasts (“You think I’m over the hill / You think I’m past my prime / Let me see what you got / We can have a whoppin’ good time”) to tender entreaties (“I could live forever / With you perfectly / You don’t ever / Have to make a fuss over me”) and solemn vows (“I’d walk through a blazing fire, baby, if I knew you was on the other side”).

The banality of many of these lines is part of what gives them their strange energy. It's from threadbare pilgrims that songs like "Nettie Moore" and "Spirit on the Water" seem to sprout — characters who need clichés as bulwarks against exhaustion and doubt. Sung with *this* sort of brittle gravity and invested with this sort of emotional need, romantic entreaties start to sound like prayers. It's hard to detect a shade of difference between the tone Dylan takes when he makes a snap religious confession midway through "Nettie Moore" — "I'm beginning to believe what the scriptures tell" — and the one that suffuses the climactic, lovesick invitation in "Spirit on the Water":

High on the hill
You can carry all my thoughts with you
You've numbed my will
This love could tear me in two

4

The first thing most critics approvingly observed about *Tempest* when the record — Dylan's most recent collection of original songs — appeared in 2012 was its violent streak. (*The Guardian* called it "murderous," *The New York Times* "wrathful" and "grim," *The New Yorker* "gruesome" and "stubbornly amoral.") Dylan never exactly went out of his way to disabuse them of that image; two weeks after the album's release, he snarled in a long, abrasive *Rolling Stone* interview — apropos of the "people that tried to pin the name Judas on me" — that "all those evil motherfuckers can rot in hell."

At the start of the same interview, Dylan hinted at his initial impulse to "make something more religious" than the record that became *Tempest*. The corners of American music to which the album's 10 songs relate most directly are, indeed, worlds away from the lamblike serenity of The Blue Sky Boys or the prayerful evocations of Washington Phillips or Homer Quincy Smith. *Tempest* occupies darker territory: a space of murder ballads, prison work songs, sinister Appalachian outlaw stories, disaster ditties, and slabs of vengeful country blues. Rock critics made much of this connection when it came to the record's two long climactic narrative songs, which vividly evoked, respectively, a triple murder-suicide ("Tin Angel") and the sinking of the Titanic (the title track).

And yet it requires some selective listening to call *Tempest* a record of murder ballads when it proceeds, for the most part, as a loose assembly of spontaneous, acidic outbursts: aggressive first-person monologues with no clear characters save the overheated singers themselves. Unconverted show-ups at a camp meeting lavishly enumerating their sins; street-corner preachers carried away by their own hellfire rants; reverends indulging in minutely imagined visions of the torments of the damned: the American character types *Tempest* maps are more religious, in at least a certain sense of the word, than Dylan has ever let on.

Who said, after all, that early gospel music had to be polite? Songs like "You'll Never Go to Heaven With Your Powder and Your Paint" by the now-forgotten duo Ira and Eugene Yates, are confrontational, vengeful, rude, and cruel. ("You'll never get to Heaven with your bobbed hair / You're going down to hell, they have a barbershop there.") Much of the appeal of recorded sermons lay in hearing charismatic preachers contort their voices into barks, grimaces, and snarls; listen, for instance, to the way "The Liar," an amazing sermon by Rev. Isaiah Shelton, rumbles out of the preacher's mouth in sonorous, condemnatory couplets, or the way the prolific Elder Richard Bryant fills out the sandpaper textures of "Saul, A Wicked Man," or the way the guitar evangelist Rev. I.B. Ware's wife and son wail hauntingly behind him as he sings a lumbering rendition of "You Better Quit Drinking Shine."

The personae these preachers and singers took on were *born* angry, their bile a righteous calling with no need for an explanatory cause; unlike the blues singers who vented similarly murderous drives, they didn't need an act of infidelity, betrayal, or injustice to sour them on humankind. It's no easier to imagine what set them off than it is to find a basis for the violent threats that fill Dylan's "Early Roman Kings" ("I can strip you of life / Strip you of breath / Ship you down / To the house of death"), to account for the unchecked fury of a song like "Pay in Blood" ("I got something in my pocket, make your eyeballs swim / I got dogs could tear you limb from limb"), or to identify the sinister, elaborately imagined setting of "Scarlet Town," where "the evil and the good livin' side by side" and "all human forms seem glorified."

The last lines of "Narrow Way" hint at the kind of conversion narrative on which many prewar gospel songs are built —

> I heard a voice at the dusk of day
> Saying, "Be gentle brother, be gentle and pray."
> It's a long road, it's a long and narrow way
> If I can't work up to you, you'll surely have to work down to me someday.

— but the song is too rabid to admit anything like a submissive religious conversion into its world. In moments like this, which occur often enough in recorded sermons and sinner testimonies, the death obsession of early gospel music — its eager interest in who would turn out "up" or "down" on the other side of life — takes a bloody, mud-splattered shape.

By 2012, Dylan was wise enough to the religious musical traditions he was riffing on to know that gospel singers didn't always work up to salvation, that they didn't always so much as claim to have heaven on their minds. Hell was on their minds too, as well as the narrow, dark, misshapen world between those two eternities. That sacred music could be loud, vulgar, disruptive, and irreverent; that it could deal in threats and taunts just as well as in pieties; that it could share a lineage with love songs and folk ballads; that it could obsess, doubt, rave, babble, fidget, and grunt in frustration; that it could emerge from the grooves of a record seemingly up to its neck in mud and earth as well as in baptismal water: Dylan's late records propose as rich and capacious a picture of old American gospel as any in popular music. The doors were there all along, on compilations like the *Anthology* and in stacks of more or less forgotten 78s. It just took this particular interpreter, with his inconstant temper, attentive ear, and loose tongue, to open them.

CODY TREPTE >
EVERYTHING HAS ALWAYS ALREADY BEGUN, 2009
INK ON PAPER; SERIES OF 30 DRAWINGS, 17 X 23" EACH
COURTESY OF THE ARTIST

EVERYTHING HAS
ALWAYS ALREADY
BEGUN

EVERYTHING HAS
ALWAYS ALREADY
BEGUN

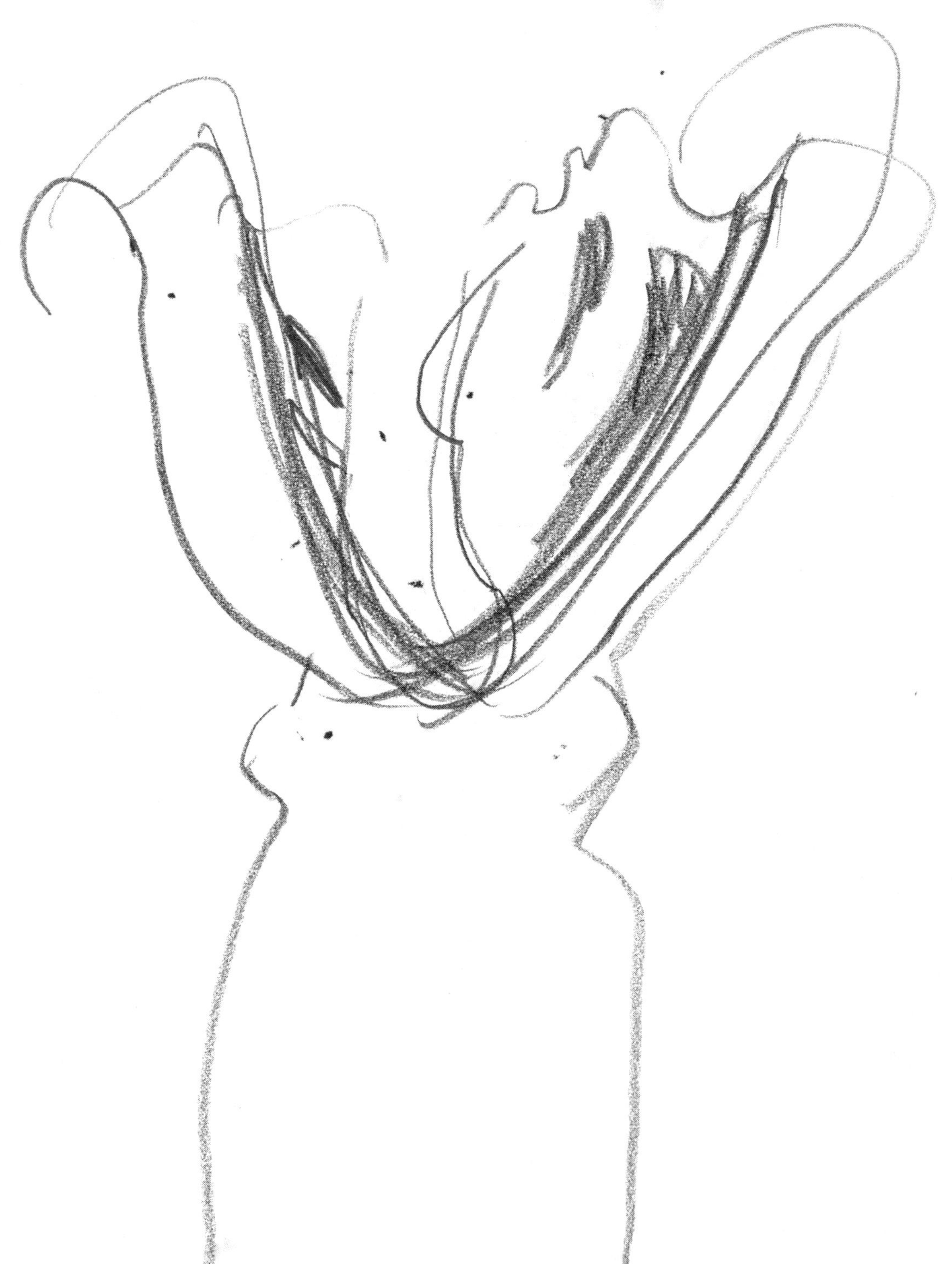

After the Birthing, the Harpia Pick the Field Clean

TRACI BRIMHALL

I arrive too late to see it, but everyone stands
at the edge of the tall grass, making wings
of their fingers – their hooked thumbs, the bodies
of harpia eagles diving to snatch the afterbirth.
New mothers lick blood from their calves' ears
as I steal a scalpel from the doctor's pocket and carve
my initials into the carousel horse. Last week I saw
a winged man robbing flowers from tombstones, or so
I tell myself to explain the embalmed angel in the mortuary.
Yesterday I clipped a black curl from the angel's thigh
to prove something to my future self about pleasure.
My new wife sleeps with her legs open, her mouth
monstrous in the grave light of morning. I paid to touch
a woman once, reached through a slit black curtain and felt
the gates of heaven stitched shut. I no longer need everything
to be possible, only the chance to believe my pleasures
could be innocent. I could follow my instincts and everyone
would live. I could wear wings, wide and weightless, and
pretend to steal afterbirth out of the eagle's crooked beak
and share it with the crowd to multiply the feast, to let
everyone lick the blood from each other's mouths
and leave, for once, sated and unharmed.

< SIMONE FORTI
SONG OF THE VOWELS, 2009
GRAPHITE AND MARKER ON PAPER, 26 5/8 X 21 1/8"
COURTESY OF THE ARTIST AND THE BOX, LA

Death SALLY ASHTON

FORTY YEARS LATER, somebody's father died, and we found each other once more (at the funeral), old schoolmates, a bit rearranged but unscathed. So we planned a weekend away, five of us from the '70s, at someone's mountain ranch. We talked, cooked, drank, looked through a surviving yearbook, hoped for glimpses of what we were. We fed cows. I slept with cricket calls, memories emerging from what had been long forgotten. In the morning I climbed to the top of a hill and turned all the way around, my circling steps in the dry grass and an occasional birdcall the only sounds. I could see for miles in any direction — sloping hills, oaks, stands of pine. Like when I was 17. After breakfast we talked about aging parents, about aging ourselves, and Buzz said he didn't like the idea of a sudden death because he wanted time to prepare for it, and I said isn't that what life is for, and he said you're right and laughed, and we all laughed, a laughter I would have known anywhere. Now in the car again, the hills that had surrounded me appear in the rearview mirror. Around a curve, they're gone. I lean in close to see past this face, to see I am still reflected there.

CODY TREPTE >
EVERYTHING HAS ALWAYS ALREADY BEGUN, 2009
INK ON PAPER; SERIES OF 30 DRAWINGS, 17 X 23" EACH
COURTESY OF THE ARTIST

EVERYTHING

EVERYTHING HAS
ALWAYS *ALREADY*
BEGUN

SANTA ANAS

LISKA JACOBS

> To live with the Santa Ana is to accept, consciously or unconsciously, a deeply mechanistic view of human behavior.
> — Joan Didion, "Los Angeles Notebook"

> The hot afternoon wore on.
> — Maritta Wolff, *Sudden Rain*

I RIDE THE EXPO LINE into downtown from Crenshaw, where our apartment is — with its bedroom window overlooking Martin Luther King Jr. Blvd. The heat is worse here than anywhere in the city, the wind incessant. At night the helicopters and sirens shriek like kettles. There are searchlights on our floors — pale, suspicious ghosts. Then a bus rattling the one window so we think it might break. The guy beneath us, who everyone calls Guy, works on the oil derricks out in the middle of the bay — he's gone for weeks at a time. When he comes home, sending the cockroaches scurrying, he tells us even the sea is boiling.

On the train the AC pumps so loud we have to turn our music way up just to hear it. It's a relief though — if we breathe through our mouths and close our eyes we could be in a museum or some cold library. Also don't touch anything. Everyone is sweating, bare limbed. When the train lurches I rub against scratchy thighs — a bit oily. This would be unacceptable if I weren't headed downtown to the bookstore, where uglier, nastier things will brush up against me. Downtown will be the human stench — their burnt leathery smell, sometimes sharp and smelling of patchouli, sometimes unmasked, the bare earthy sourness between belly folds and underarms — the backs of legs, the unwashed hair, the acrid stench of human roasting.

When the doors open at 7th and Metro, I climb the stairs with everyone else. The air in the tunnels is already breathy — like being in the belly of some slumbering beast — but outside the sidewalks are blistery. It's the kind of heat that socks you right in the face. The wind would almost be a relief if it didn't drive everyone half-mad. The women on street corners, breasts spilling out of their tops, fight with anyone who looks at them sideways — I've seen them push people in front of cars. And then there are the men who lie on the sidewalks, shoeless, feet dark and crusty, pulled up almost to their stomachs like a baby in utero. They look at you, really eye you, faces pockmarked and dogged — these are the broken faces of those who sleep, eat, live here, down in the dirt — weary of change because change never brought them anything good.

My job at the bookstore is to buy books. It's a new and used store, and we get most of our used books from the public. We wear gloves because when it's hot like this the bugs come out — and because books are never stored anywhere pleasant. It's always the garage or shed with rats and mold. The silverfish are first, and we squash them with a stapler. Then, spiders small like ants or sometimes so large we see hair on their backs. For some reason the big spiders — some the size of a silver dollar — are not very quick, only moving when the shadow of the stapler comes down and splat. It's the baby cockroaches we watch out for; they are quick — quick enough to run up a gloved hand, onto a bare arm.

After work my husband and I don't go home. We wait until it's cooled down. We are expert waiters. First while working on bachelor degrees — two community colleges — then it was off to San Luis Obispo for him while I continued at UCLA. When he took a year off, got a job at a fancy pizza restaurant, we waited while paying down credit card debt one month at a time. Then it was waiting through CSUN, the three years he spent driving the impossible 405 — up and down, back and forth. He waits now for a raise, a better job. And me, waiting for my writing to take off, for that one publication where something might change.

So we're good at waiting, and we wait as long as possible before going home. We don't want the hot chicken skin smell coming from Ralphs, how it rides the thin wind easier than anything. We don't want to open the door to the stale air, the cheap paint and carpet smells. To find American cockroaches — bigger than their German counterparts, they crawl out from the pipes to die under the furniture. We don't want to see the ring of Ajax around the bed, or where our couch used to be. Once, after a long day, we came home to find them hiding between the cushions — only hiding isn't the right word. They were reigning, *lording*, over the couch. That couch is in the alley now.

Instead, we drive to Pasadena or out to Santa Monica, to the groomed lawns, the immaculate properties that come with privilege. In these neighborhoods we close our eyes, listen to sprinklers. When was the last rain? Look at this picture of Lake Shasta, look how the boats sit clustered in the center of what appears to be a dry salt bed. All of California is bright red on the weather maps — it looks painfully chapped. Maybe there will be rain in the spring.

We go to a happy hour — any happy hour, as long as it's air-conditioned, with cheap strong drinks. At Islands, we drink tropical cocktails and eat what the bar menu calls "street tacos." A fight breaks out in the parking lot between a man and a woman. The woman pushes her flat open palm in the man's face. She curls her fingers a little, scraping at the skin. The wind scatters leaf litter and debris around their tousled legs. This feels surreal to us, like it's happened before. *Pinch me*, I tell my husband. *I'm having déjà vu.*

We toss and turn at the apartment, one or both of us taking a sleeping pill. Then we wake and my husband heads west on the Expo Line to his design job and I head east to downtown. We ride the trains with their roaring AC and bare limbs and smells of sweet yeast — too much human flesh. One day there will be more than this, we tell ourselves, *Just wait …*

At the bookstore again, the fans are switched to high. We keep the windows closed. Sometimes we hear the wind whistle against them. We take our lunch breaks indoors because outside nerves flash. There have been two suicides downtown this week. They go into the tunnels, jump in front of the Red Line train as it pulls into Pershing Square. We see paramedics and police lights from the store. The customers get skittish and stay away. The regulars who come up from Skid Row smell worse on days like these. We check the weather forecast on our phones 12 days at a time. Winds again, record digits.

Just after lunch I see a woman in her 40s crossing Spring Street with her mother. They've braved the heat and wind and borrowed a dolly, and as I look the wind picks up, sending the mother's skirt twisting. The mother says her daughter's husband has died suddenly, would we like to look at the books? And then they come, 10, 12 boxes, and we go through every box. Here is his Boy Scout manual, his books on space and rocks, annotated in the margin in a careful hand. There are army and philosophy books, big coffee-table books on movies and Monet, travel books on Southeast Asia and Europe with tickets and receipts stuffed between the pages. A collection of encyclopedias, made worthless by water damage and age — Czechoslovakia still on the world map. And relationship books, too — *How to Satisfy Her*, *How to Be a Better Husband*. *The Complete Idiot's Guide to Kama Sutra*. Books on Photoshop and how to build a web page, Twitter and the stock market. We are sweating and when we reach the bottom and silverfish crawl out we do not jump. We step on them casually.

There are the usual classics: Hemingway and Nabokov and a few slim volumes of Rilke, which we put aside to buy. All in all we can't offer much, I think it's less than 60 dollars. The widow starts crying immediately. She too has sweated through her blouse; I can see the beige Maidenform bra with its tiny bows at the shoulders. *It's the wind, the damn wind*, her mother tells us over and over. We offer water, find a chair. The widow sits and cries while we pay the mother, who folds the receipt to fit as if her wallet were a tiny coffin with a zipper. They donate the rest of the books and we throw most of them away. Some go up to the dollar room. It's a sad thing, when you can survey a life — its systematic orbit — in one afternoon. Will this happen to us I wonder? It must — but what will we have if we wait too long, letting weeks slip into months. Has it been a year already? Where did 2015 go?

I take the Boy Scout notebook home with me. In a young unsure hand the dead man has charted the stars. I ride the train thinking that tonight there will be a brief reprieve from the wind. My husband and I will sit on our deck, facing eucalyptus trees where feral green parrots have gathered, chased out of San Diego by the fires. We won't mind their noise; it will drown out the buses and music and brake sounds that rise up from the boulevard. We'll drink iced cranberry juice with vodka, tense at anything that crawls or flies. Guy will have come home from the derricks; we'll hear Sade from his apartment below. Every once in a while he'll croon along, *When am I gonna make a living, Ohhh …*

We'll point out Andromeda, Ursa Minor to each other, guess at Jupiter — the sky clear and large and infinite. We'll talk about starlight, how it travels millions of years to reach us — how short and long time can be. Then the neighbor's dog will begin to bark, and a whole chorus of dogs will soon join in. We'll feel it in our sinuses, a slight tickle. A rustling high up in the treetops, a hot thin swell that slides over and under, round and round, another Santa Ana on its way.

CODY TREPTE >
EVERYTHING HAS ALWAYS ALREADY BEGUN, 2009
INK ON PAPER; SERIES OF 30 DRAWINGS, 17 X 23" EACH
COURTESY OF THE ARTIST

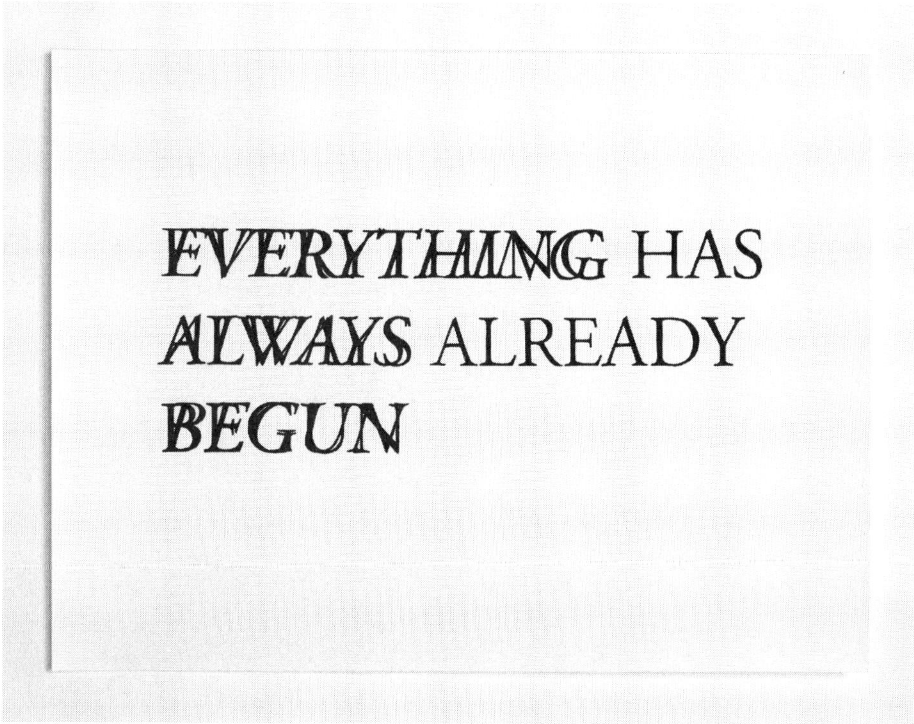

EVERYTHING HAS
ALWAYS ALREADY
BEGUN

EVERYTHING HAS
ALWAYS ALREADY
BEGUN

Invention of Thunder

DIANE SEUSS

I was Freddie Mercury's body. I was the recording studio inside his mouth. His horse teeth were the teeth of my stallion. The show saddle that rubbed my thighs was tooled with scenes of Freddie's early life in Zanzibar. He never fixed his teeth because he didn't want to fuck up his voice. I never fixed my voice because I didn't want to fuck up my teeth. The cow eye I dissected before I learned to be squeamish was his Adam's apple. Freddie's wardrobe was my uncle-by-marriage's fly-by-night mink farm. Freddie's waistcoat painted with pictures of his cats was a cage filled with condemned minks. His cats bred a stillborn black kitten who took up residence between my thighs. Freddie's mustache was my smuggled buffalo. His mustache was my armpit shag. His high note was my low note. His high note set off tornado sirens and wedding bells. Freddie's last thought knocked out my bowling alley. His last T cell apocalypsed my funeral parlor until the embalming table rattled off its runners.

Memory Fed Me Until It Didn't

DIANE SEUSS

Then the erotic charge turned off like a light switch.
I think the last fire got peed on in that hotel outside Lansing.
Peed and sizzled and then a welcome and lasting silence.

Then my eyes got hungry.
They looked at bowls and barn owls and paper clips,
panoramic lavender fields and a single purple spear

and it was good but not good enough.
My eyes were hungry for paint, like I used to imagine
a horse could taste the green in its mouth

before its lips found the grass.
Then I woke to the words "still life," not as the afterimage
of a dream but as the body wakes and knows it needs

mince pie before the mind has come to claim it.
I craved paint like the pregnant body craves pomegranates
or hasenpfeffer or that sauerbraten made with gingersnaps.

Van Gogh ate paint. At least that's the myth of van Gogh.
I ate van Gogh, the still lives of old boots and thick-tongued
irises. Then my eyes followed the trail back, to Dürer

and his plump rabbit, as perfectly composed as a real one,
as if he'd invented rabbits, and Chardin's dead hare
strung up in a brownish-gold space, its head and ears

flopped on what appears to be a table, the ears
made of rough bands of white and black and gray
and green-brown paint, the whiskers painted in, the tufts

of fur articulated with white gestures from a thin brush.
And the vanitas paintings, of skulls and unspent coins,
and Baugin's dessert wafers shaped like little flutes,

and Pieter Aertsen's "The Butcher's Stall,"
in which a small rendering of the Holy Family on the Flight
into Egypt is relegated to the background,

while the foreground is loaded with gaudy carnage,
a vat of lard, a pig's head hung by the snout, cascades
of sausages, strangled hens, and yawning sides of beef.

The huge gory head of a cow is front and center,
directly below the cool blues of the miniature Virgin Mary
handing out alms to the poor. The cow's cold nose

is so close it makes my eyes water. Its watery eye
gazes back at me and I fall in love. I fall in love again. ///

CODY TREPTE >
EVERYTHING HAS ALWAYS ALREADY BEGUN, 2009
INK ON PAPER; SERIES OF 30 DRAWINGS, 17 X 23" EACH
COURTESY OF THE ARTIST

EVERYTHI

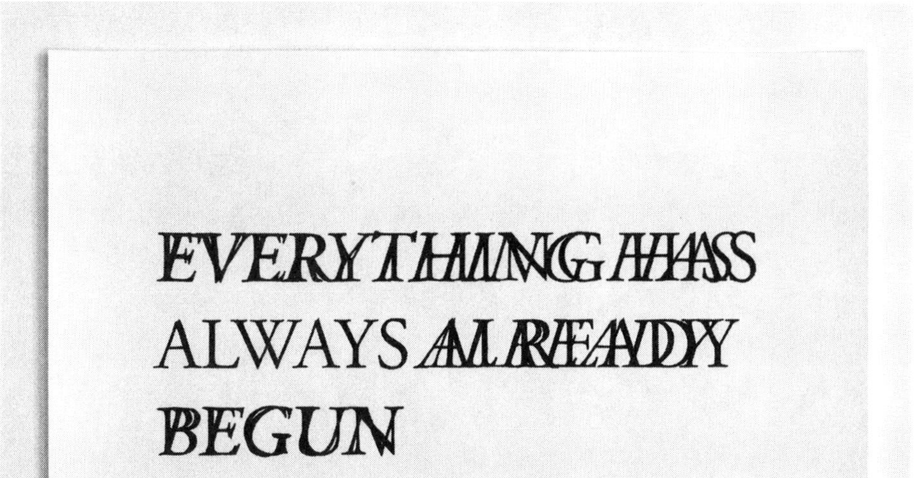

EVERYTHING HAS
ALWAYS ALREADY
BEGUN

ANISSA MACK
UNTITLED, 2009
PAINTED ALUMINUM; 17 1/2 X 9 X 7 1/2"
COURTESY OF THE ARTIST AND LAUREL GITLEN, NEW YORK

Panic KIM YOUNG

WE'RE IN MY CAR PEAKING on acid. My sister, in the front on the passenger side, is singing along to PJ Harvey's "Rub 'til It Bleeds." And by singing along, I mean she has grown larger than her muscular frame — she's moaning like PJ, and she's communicating something primal, some energetic hum, some essential version of herself.

"Holy shit," I say to Erin. We're in the backseat. Our eyeballs are black. It's like we can see. Finally.

And you believe meeeeeee, screams PJ.

Erin grabs my hand. Josh Murphy is driving. He pulls my car into one of those corner mini-mall lots. I'm wearing a full-length faux fur coat from the Salvation Army over my Dickies and men's cardigan. I'm wearing Adidas. My lips are very chapped. Inside 7-Eleven, I pull down a stiff lever and watch as cherry Slurpee pours into my cup.

Ding-dong. In walk two cops. LAPD. In full jangly black uniform.

By the time we're tripping on acid in my car, my sister is two, maybe three years past the night she snuck out of the house to meet Atti at *The Rocky Horror Picture Show*. The night the man in the Ford Bronco pulled a gun to get her in the car. She's three years past the things that happened inside that Ford Bronco, before he dropped her off at the supermarket with change.

Now, years later, sitting in the backseat with Erin, my sister rises in front of us like some unfurling. It's our adolescence. We crank up the song while we drive past the silent hedges — past all these streets that seemed normal once, you know, or safe, at least.

In the 7-Eleven, though, the equipment hums, and even if I couldn't actually hear the cops' footsteps, I imagined that I could. I knew that car was idling in the parking lot just outside. I knew PJ was still singing. My sister was lighting a cigarette. Josh was asking Erin why we bought that pack of nasty bidis from India Sweets & Spices.

I'm calling you weak.

I lean into the door of the 7-Eleven and make it out without one of the cops placing a hand on my shoulder. I slide into the backseat of the car with my Slurpee while Josh carefully flips on the turn signal to responsibly indicate his intention to make a right turn. The car smells like smoke and bodies. I'm usually the driver of my own car but being there in the backseat gives me a vantage point by which I never see my sister. She's looking toward the windshield, and I'm behind her. I watch her light a cigarette, smile at Josh, and then finally turn back to us. She's still singing along with PJ, and I can tell by her expression that she knows. She knows I can see it — that part of her that's wailing with a wild black voice and something bigger than anything that breaks inside of her or inside of anyone.

SOCHI, 2014

PAUL MANDELBAUM

DAY TWO OF THE GAMES, Putin spied a potential threat across the luge: a brunette who kept fiddling with her ski vest, its odd bulge suggesting hidden explosives. Maybe that was paranoid. After all, she had good Slavic cheekbones. On the other hand, nothing got a man blown to bits faster in this world than thinking with his *khuy*. He was about to signal his nearest FSB officer, when the woman's bosom began to quiver and there emerged, from her zipper's cleft, the whiskered snout of a small dog.

Who would dare smuggle an animal past presidential security? So brazen was the act, it could hardly fail to impress him. Only after the danger had passed did his pulse begin to race, and he smiled at the response she'd provoked in him, she with her little dog. Wasn't there a Chekhov story about a lady with a lapdog at a seaside resort, where she awakens the heart of a distinguished older man? He should probably read it again.

A sled shot past, but he ignored it to study the woman's mouth. She plucked at her lower lip, and her expression played the edge between hope and despair, which became for Putin the more interesting competition. Each time another pair of lugers rushed by, she rose on the balls of her feet, a habit he found charming, until she appeared to take special interest in the Ukrainian national team.

At that point, having other events to attend, he left. But the woman with the dog stayed until every last sled had run its course. She then strolled to a Tatar café, where she offered bits of dumpling to the animal still sheltered against her breast before returning to the Radisson Lazurnaya at precisely 17:49.

The next day, as he waited to learn whether she would join him for tea, Putin faced a number of decisions only he could make. With all eyes on Sochi, Russia could ill afford missteps that would be amplified by the world media. The producer of Friday's opening ceremonies was led into the room, his tailored shirt dark with sweat. Putin had yet to forgive that fifth Olympic ring, whose faulty

PIETER SCHOOLWERTH
AFTER TROY 1, 2012
OIL, ACRYLIC, GICLÉE PRINT AND OIL PASTEL ON CANVAS; 73 X 54"
COURTESY THE ARTIST AND MIGUEL ABREU GALLERY, NEW YORK; PHOTO: JEFFREY STURGES

pyrotechnics failed to make it bloom. Such humiliation for the Motherland, a global declaration of impotence. *I'm very sorry, Mr. President, a damaged wire, Mr. President* — "If you do that again ..." Here Putin paused, savoring the man's discomfort, until finally proposing a solution: "If you do that again on the final night, the world will appreciate our sense of humor." The producer laughed, but with such strangled pain, it was clear he had no idea whether Putin was joking.

On the phone, his finance minister whimpered about the Ukrainian bailout. *Of course, Mr. President, you're correct to maintain our influence, but 15 billion* — "Then link it to their gas debt." Putin had promised Kiev aid enough to quell the growing unrest in its public Maidan, all that hatred toward its leader, and, more importantly, toward neighboring Russia. It was the very last turmoil he needed right now.

Throughout the morning, he kept thinking about Sonia from the luge. That was her name, according to a hastily assembled dossier: Sonia Ivanovna Shevchenko — 33 years, 165 centimeters, Peter-born but married to a Ukrainian. No history of political tendencies or even a single vote. She'd earned half the units toward a mathematics degree, but worked as a bookkeeper in her husband's family business, a cannery in the Crimean town of Kerch. They had no children.

The married part was problematic, but Putin could not stop pondering her outrageous display of cheek, and fantasized she might offer something beyond the blind obedience women assumed he wanted. Indeed, when she arrived at the compound later that afternoon, her dog perched on one hip, Sonia Ivanovna demanded whether it had been strictly necessary, moments earlier by the entrance, to subject the animal to a full-body scan.

"I'm afraid," he replied, "my security chief tends to err on the side of caution." Having a way with dogs, he presented his fingertips, and Maxim, as the creature was named, licked them. "We have tea and blinis. Also water," added Putin, who had thought to provide a bowl. "Please, make yourself comfortable." Dismissing his aide, he poured Sonia and himself each a cup of tea, then joined her on the deerskin couch.

She'd removed the infamous vest that had got his heart racing yesterday. Without the padding of her dog, her bosom lay almost flat and yet still exerted a theatrical pull on his imagination. She wore no jewelry, beyond a plain wedding band so thin it could have been a toy. Glancing downward, she accepted a sugar cube from the dish he held out to her, then hid it against the inside of her cheek. Putin did likewise.

"Naughty boy," she mumbled, as she tried to shoo Maxim off the couch, then explained, "He has separation anxiety and refuses to be alone."

"It's fine." Patting his lap, Putin persuaded the dog to nest there, then asked a question whose answer he already knew: *Where were her people from?* "Peter, like yourself," she said, having since moved to Crimea to be with her husband. *And had he joined her on this trip?* No, Mykola stayed behind to run his parents' cannery, a business he'd grown from almost nothing and now obsessed over. *Did she herself work there?* Until recently, she'd managed the front office, but was making herself "take a break."

"A break." He spoke around the bit of sweetness in his mouth and asked if she planned to return home right after the games. "Or will your break extend beyond?"

"I'm not sure."

"Well, I'm grateful you chose to spend some of your break at our Olympics." Putin could not stop saying the word *break*, which had begun to sound like code for something fragile about her marriage.

"The games seemed a good place to watch people trying their best," she said, and this too sounded like a veiled comment on her husband and their life in Crimea.

"I couldn't help notice, you were rooting for the Ukrainian lugers."

She straightened against the cushions. "What makes you say so?"

"It could not have been more obvious! Do you no longer think of yourself as Russian first?"

"To be honest, I don't know whom I'm supposed to root for." Her eyes softened, and so bereft did she appear in that moment, he tried to cheer her with a little joke.

"That's a shame," he said. "I myself am rooting for Russia."

It was a good simple joke, and he'd managed not to overdo it. Another woman might have blinked dumbly or howled like a loon, but Sonia Ivanovna rewarded him with a knowing smile, and he was impressed by the perfect scale of her response. He would probe a little deeper into her politics. "What do you make of the ruckus in your so-called capital, that circus overtaking the public Maidan?"

"I have no stomach for conflict." She seemed sad to admit this, and yet her steady gaze challenged him.

"You must realize," he said, "joining the EU would hardly fix all Ukraine's problems."

"Maybe so," she allowed, but the ambiguity of her reply frustrated him.

"Sonia Ivanovna, surely you don't wish to become a pawn of the West?"

"Whose pawn would you have me be?" She blurted this with an asperity that felt, much to his delight, like a fingernail drawn along the length of his spine. Meanwhile, however, a look of mortification had befallen her. "Please forgive my rudeness."

"There's nothing to forgive," he insisted, her apology of no use to him. "By all means, speak your mind." But having grown shy, she just smoothed the hem of her dress. "Yesterday you were so bold," he reminded her, "smuggling your dog past a security cordon. May I ask what for?"

"Honestly, I couldn't say. My heart was pounding. So maybe that."

"Would joining me tomorrow as my guest seem anticlimactic?" He tried to wink, but his lid clenched, as though a gnat had flown into his eye, and the joke was spoiled.

"I probably shouldn't," she murmured, a private thought spoken out loud. "My husband might be watching on television."

"Along with the rest of the world!" He resented her insinuation that some moral line had been crossed, and a silence grew between them. Before long, he summoned his aide to escort her out. "It's been a pleasure," Putin said, handing back her dog.

Sonia Ivanovna remained silent until they reached the door to his study, at which point she said, "I would like to join you tomorrow. If the invitation still holds."

Did she suddenly favor the idea of making her husband jealous? That was not the role Putin envisioned for himself, but rescinding the offer would lack class. "Very well," he said. "Be sure to bring Maxim, since he refuses to be alone."

The next day he took her to the biathlon, where they enjoyed a view of the shooting range obstructed by nothing more than 50 millimeters of German-made glass. Even that modest barrier he felt a sudden impulse to remove, and not just because it came from the West. While he understood his duty to stay safe for the Russian people, what about his right to enjoy life? Standing close to Sonia Ivanovna, he inhaled the scent of her skin and tried to identify its pleasing zest. Like caraway. As he extolled the technology and sheer human will required to ensure an adequate snowpack, she gave him another of those knowing smiles he'd already developed a taste for. Naturally, she had brought Maxim. No longer obliged to hide him beneath her vest, she maybe should have, because the animal grew more fidgety with each gunshot.

"Wouldn't your husband have looked after him back home?"

"Mykola? No, my husband is always vowing to get rid of him. Never trust a man who doesn't like dogs."

Putin realized he'd been fishing for a fuller sense of her marriage, and in fact the union did not seem healthy. Maybe even in its last days. Maxim meanwhile continued to squirm against her grasp. Just as the lead skiers unsheathed their rifles and commenced another round of shots, the little dog leapt from her arms and immediately slipped through a gap in the bleacher boards. Unable to pursue him, Sonia pressed her forehead against the bulletproof glass, the helpless sight of which roused in Putin a protective impulse, as her dog barreled through the snow toward the rifle range.

"Maxim!" she called, rapping with her toy ring.

"Please calm yourself, Sonia Ivanovna."

With a tight nod, Putin signaled his lead man on the field, who in three strides reached the little dog and scooped him up. Within seconds, Maxim was returned to his frantic owner, who swaddled him under her vest and gently scolded him, her head bent at such an intimate angle she appeared to address herself. "Naughty thing. Stirring trouble."

"You see," Putin said, "everything's been made fine."

She wheeled to face him, her expression wavering once again between hope and despair, and asked if they could leave.

"As you like," he said, the biathlon having lost its luster. "Should I drop you at the Radisson?" But Sonia Ivanovna would sooner, she at last made clear, return with him to the presidential compound, where they might be alone. Though his common sense raged against it, Putin enjoyed a delicious sense of anticipation.

As soon as they entered his study, she leaned against him, closed her eyes, and pointed her mouth toward his. How conscious was she of herself in that moment, or of him? Sometimes Putin wondered if true consent were even possible toward someone as formidable as he. Did it matter to anyone who he was inside, or had his own power made access to that man impossible?

"What's wrong?" she asked. "Don't you want to kiss me?"

"Sonia Ivanovna." He proceeded to crack open a door that maybe should have remained closed: "What about your husband?"

Noticing Maxim against her hip, she set him down in order to shed her vest, after which she described a marriage full of regrets, akin to prison. She should never have dropped out of school for her husband's sake, and last month she'd found him in bed with a girl from the cannery line. "Barely 17, this girl. Still pimpled on her backside. Also, pink toenails." Each demeaning detail made Sonia wilt.

"Are you seeking a way out?" Maybe she just needed a benefactor to arrange a soft landing. If so, he would help, but only if she asked.

Fatigued, she slumped onto the deerskin couch. "It's all so complicated."

Was it really though? His own divorce had been perfectly civil, as he'd stressed to the media. Of course, that didn't mean it had left him unscathed. Having known his former wife through most of adulthood, he felt as though an entire side of his experience had calved from him like a glacier. Sometimes he forgot whose idea it had first been to part.

"Eat something," he urged.

"Better you should take me to bed," she said, in a voice less bold than her words.

Putin thought a moment, then led her by the hand to his private quarters. Once there, however, he opened the bureau dresser and withdrew a pair of his own flannel pajamas.

"When you awake," he said, handing them to her, "we'll see how badly you still want to kiss me."

Back in his study, he took a call from Yanukovych, his beleaguered counterpart in Ukraine, who pretended to thank him for the announced debt relief but suggested a cash show of support might do more to stop the tire fires in Maidan square.

"I'll tap another billion or two," said Putin. "Don't dare spend it on yourself."

"I've learned my lesson, Vladimir Vladimirovich. Thank you from the bottom of my heart."

"Let's hope your people don't rip it from your chest."

Yanukovych brayed like he'd just heard the best joke in the world. *Idiot*, Putin muttered soon after hanging up. Curled nearby on the deerskin couch, Maxim lifted his head to nibble a dab of sour cream from Putin's fingertip. In the two hours Sonia had been napping, he'd taught the dog to roll over, fetch a presidential pen, and balance a paperback biography of Ivan the so-called Terrible. A voice now chimed from the doorway. "Again he escaped?" Looking up, Putin saw she still wore his pajamas and, though he might have wished the arms to hang longer on her, he otherwise found the sight endearing. Her nap had done her good. She seemed calmer now, no longer so at odds with herself.

"I required his presence for an important phone call with your president."

"Is that so?" she said with flirtatious ease.

Putin was wondering if she even considered Yanukovych her president at all, or just a placeholder until Crimea could be someday restored to Mother Russia. Then he noticed her face closing in on his. Her lips, slightly chapped, pressed against him with insistence, and her tongue ranged back and forth over his.

Soon they repaired to his private quarters. After settling Maxim on a blanket in the anteroom, the two of them undressed each other, shy all of a sudden. Though he kept in shape, the age difference was stark and prompted him to suggest they climb beneath the covers. Kissing her navel, he sought the source of her caraway scent, as she clutched his hand, her lips arranging a constellation of little chapped kisses across his palm. Only as he entered her did Putin wonder if he hadn't made a naive error, though surely at this point in his career, no blackmail threat could touch him. He opened his eyes to see tears glazing her cheeks.

"What's the matter?"

"I'm fine," she said, clearly not. Withdrawing, he spooned behind her and stroked her belly in a soothing manner. At least, he found it so himself. He hadn't simply lain with a woman, in stillness like this, for ages. He spoke into her hair: "Why don't you stay for supper."

"I'd like that, but I should return to the hotel. My husband expects to Skype."

"The two of you Skype."

Apologetically she said, "Each evening, at six."

How had his people neglected to inform him? The status of her marriage seemed more ambiguous all of a sudden, wooing her quite ill-advised. And yet, as he watched her step into her own clothes, withdrawing her nakedness, he heard himself ask to see her the next day. "Please think about it," he said, entrusting her with the number to his private line.

Insomnia spun him like a top, as he wondered what she wanted of him, or he of her. At this point in life, he hardly expected grand romance. Those were the fantasies of a schoolboy, not the leader of a great nation. In his mind all of a sudden rang the offensive phrase *leader of the free world*. By what right, he often wondered, did Americans call their president such a thing? As though Russians would only follow a master, with no real love for him in their hearts. How superior Obama had sounded, voicing his hope for a Ukrainian government "with greater legitimacy and unity," since the present one, disposed toward Moscow, could not possibly claim either.

The next day, circles under his eyes, Putin spent a glum morning listening to his advisers peddle frantic predictions should Russia lose control over its partner-state, as though Ukraine were a disloyal spouse. Such an insult could not be tolerated, everyone agreed, but the solution was left to him. In fairness, that's what he preferred, though just then it gave him a stabbing headache. Keen to clear his mind, Putin left to make an appearance at the men's speed skating. The event was so dominated by Dutchmen, however, his gloom only deepened. Not until the ride back, just as his motorcade pulled into the driveway and he'd written off ever hearing from Sonia Ivanovna, did she finally call.

"Well, you missed some tremendous skating," he chided, before extending another invitation to supper. "Or will you have to rush off again like Cinderella?"

"No, I can stay," she said with great solemnity, as though she'd weighed the matter all day. "Mykola never rang last night, so to hell with that."

Putin was delighted. "I'll have a car come round at six sharp," he proposed, adding, "you may rely on it."

During supper, they shared the stories of their day. With more candor this time, Putin vented his frustration over the afternoon's skating when, to his surprise, she picked a fight about it. "Must Russia win all the medals?" she argued. "Is international esteem not the bigger prize?" She was right, of course, and her sympathetic intelligence he found at once attractive and a little unnerving. Beneath the table, he slipped Maxim a morsel of hake. Meanwhile, Sonia recounted an afternoon of writing postcards to her parents and cousins. Putin nodded, having already been briefed as much, when suddenly she said,

"Don't worry. I didn't mention you."

Only now did he think to worry. "What would you have written?" he asked. "Were you to describe me as a man."

She studied him across the table. "I'd tell everyone how gentle you can be."

Her appraisal astonished him. Had she recognized a truth so few had cared to, or did she simply bring it out in him? When they retired to bed that evening, he took extra care to live up to her assessment and managed this time not to make her weep. More encouraging yet, come morning she remained in his embrace. Gazing down, he saw, sprouted from her left areola, a lone brown hair, and found himself deeply moved. He blew on it, watching it flutter, until she awoke and plucked it from herself with a sigh of distaste.

"But why?" he asked, sorry to have shamed her.

"My body shouldn't have more hair than yours." As she ran a hand across his chest, he couldn't tell if she'd meant to mock him. But just then he hoped so, determined to take it as a sign of familiarity and hence affection.

"The larger the better," he told Yanukovych, urging the Ukrainian president to honor an impending prisoner amnesty. "Tomorrow is St. Valentine's Day, so-called."

"I don't follow. St. Valentine?"

"Why not make a big-hearted gesture, Viktor Fedorovych?" With rare patience, Putin took pity on his dense interlocutor. "Before it's too late."

Just as he hung up, Sonia returned from the lavatory. "Too late for what?"

"For your president to keep his job." Putin had planned to take the morning flurry of calls in private, but decided at the last minute to avail himself of her company. She had spent the night again, having returned to the Radisson just long enough to pick up clean clothes, and now lay her head in his lap, Maxim curled atop hers.

She said, "I have such dark feelings about that man."

Though it pleased him to hear her views, Putin felt obliged to mention, in terms she might appreciate, that as long as her Crimean town remained under Ukrainian control — the unforeseen consequence, he'd remind her, of internal Soviet-era deal-making — it was vital to keep an ally in charge. "Where would you have us dock our Black Sea fleet, if not Sevastopol?"

"Your ally," she countered, "seems poised to butcher everyone."

"And whom might you prefer in the job?" Putin asked, steering their talk away from butchery. "Tymoshenko? Or do you like the Chocolate King?"

"That part makes no difference to me. Mykola likes the Chocolate King. As a businessman, I think, my husband admires him."

"Sonia Ivanovna, would it be too much if I asked you to not mention him so often?"

She glanced up. "I don't mean to make you uncomfortable. Believe me, my situation makes me uncomfortable, too."

"And yet it needn't be your situation," he pointed out. "You are in no actual prison. You're free to leave at any time."

"I don't feel particularly free." She closed her eyes, and Putin stroked her hair as he watched her drift into a nap. Minsk was on the line, but he told his aide to take a message.

As a Valentine's Day surprise, Putin had vetted a Tatar chef and brought the man over just to fry Sonia a plate of *chiburekki*. She gasped at their flakiness, as though Putin had performed a magic trick, and was so touched by his gesture, the moment they returned to his personal quarters, she cornered him against the bath doorway and peppered his neck and ear with kisses. In the few days since their first coupling, they'd achieved a gradual comfort with each other's body, and he now lay her across the heated marble floor. Later, while soaking together in the tub, he mused, "We should christen every room in the compound."

"So many rooms." She sighed with seeming contentment, and the following afternoon decided to collect a few more of her things from the Radisson, including some of Maxim's toys. "He can't live without his Super-Ball."

Impulsively, Putin asked if she wouldn't just prefer to check out of the hotel altogether. "It's such an unnecessary expense for you."

"Mykola can pay with his last dime!" A scowl of fury had overtaken her, and she seemed as alarmed by it as he. "Sorry, I didn't mean to say his name again."

"Please, dear Sonia. Let my staff fetch your things."

But she resisted, as though the offer impugned her liberty to come and go. And Putin, not wishing to make demands, dropped it and had a car brought around for her.

Meetings. Phone calls. Decision upon decision, each an emergency Putin alone could resolve. Ukraine's prisoner amnesty having done little to calm the hatred flaring in Kiev, Putin felt obliged to throw more cash at the economy. *And what of those St. George-ists?* his defense minister asked. Recently a group of counterprotesters, wearing the Russian military ribbon of St. George and calling themselves "Kievans for a Clean City," had begun overturning the Maidan barricades. *We don't want anyone*, his minister fretted, *to think they're acting on our behalf.*

"As though we police the world's taste in ribbons!" At moments like these, when the minutest event threatened global embarrassment, Putin wondered why any sane person would be in charge. So, it came as a relief when he was asked to the east vestibule to settle a conflict that in no likely way concerned the fate of nations. Sonia Ivanovna, having returned to the compound, refused this time to subject Maxim to the body scanner. Six FSB agents had gathered to address this crisis, including Levkov himself.

"Mr. President, I keep telling her it's perfectly safe." The portly chief meandered back and forth across the machine's threshold, as though it were a fashion runway.

"It's senseless and harmful," she cried. "Would you scan an infant?"

"Mr. President, please," cautioned Levkov. "I urge you not to make exceptions."

They waited for him to speak, and Putin, weary suddenly from years of constant vigilance, reached around the scanner's side so she could pass him her dog. The small creature was trembling, as was Sonia herself and, most noticeably of all, poor Levkov, who no doubt feared going down in history for failing to perform his duty.

"A life without exceptions," Putin tried to assure everyone, not least of all himself, "is hardly worth living."

Over the next 48 hours, their intimacy only deepened. It was a time of relative peace, domestic and abroad, though of course that couldn't last, tranquility being willing to pay no more than brief visits to the restive human soul. On Tuesday, riot erupted on Kiev's Maidan. The images were shocking, for Putin none so much as that of a young girl prying bricks from Hrushevskoho Street. He pictured such a scene unfolding in Red Square someday, Muscovites dismantling the city to hurl at the very authorities who'd kept it safe and clean. Anxious to replace this image with one more pleasant, Putin went to check on Sonia in the hope they might christen a new room with their lovemaking. Instead, he found her dressing to leave again.

"What now?" He tried to sound playful. "Are we out of those little chew treats?"

Sonia insisted on returning to the hotel in order to Skype with her husband. "Not for long," she promised. "To make sure he's safe."

"The man's far from danger. Crimea's barely in Ukraine."

"Exactly right, he's a Ukrainian surrounded by Russians."

She would not listen to reason. Putin even offered to enable her cell phone to Skype from the compound. But she seemed driven to proceed on her own terms.

"Is there nothing," she asked, "you can do to make it stop?"

"Alas, those protesters are very stubborn."

"I mean," she said, "the snipers."

There had in fact been reports of rooftop snipers opening fire on the Maidan below, but Putin could discuss only so much with her. He vowed to look into it, then tried to mollify her with a kiss, but she would not be detained.

The moment she drove off, he experienced a fist in his chest, foolish jealousy posing as angina. Determined to focus, he returned some calls. Warsaw and Bucharest, as well as the chairman of his own Duma, all sought reassurance Russia was not calling the shots, so to speak, at Maidan. Germany and France wanted a word. One by one he spoke to all the major heads of state, as well as some who hadn't bothered to make contact since his last inauguration. Everybody brimmed with advice and judgment. On and on they went. The Olympics not even done, the world could hardly wait to deny Russia her moment of glory. Humanity's ill will — sometimes he feared nothing would survive it. At one point, Obama himself deigned to phone, during which the American president threatened the West's intention to sanction Ukraine come morning.

"We must each follow the demands of his conscience," said Putin, fiercely squeezing Maxim's Super-Ball. Looking up, he saw one of his aides roll a luggage cart toward the private quarters, and soon Sonia stood in the doorway, her dog tucked under one arm, at which point Putin cut short his exchange with the leader of the so-called free world in order to greet this far more attractive development.

"So!" Feeling victorious, even a bit cocksure, he said, "You decamped the Radisson."

"I wanted to make the most of our time." She smiled, but an incisor caught along her lip, and there lurked a subtext to her words, an emphasis on the transient.

"Can I assume your husband is alright, protected by only his child-mistress?"

Ignoring his sarcasm, she confessed, "I offered to fly home early. It feels wrong to desert him at a time like this. But he insists I'm safer here in Sochi."

"Of course you are! You could not possibly be safer." Jealousy again squeezed his chest, and after they'd retired to the private quarters, he steeled himself to ask, "Dear Sonia, how are you viewing our —" Here he clasped his hands together. "Connection?"

"What about you?" Her smile was sweet but tentative. "It's hard to suppose you've imagined our happiness lasting more than a few days."

"And if I were to imagine it?"

Turning toward the window, she appeared in profile genuinely confused. She dragged her teeth across her lower lip, as though to gather the right words. "I had just been thinking, on my way back here, how the sweetness between us has made life bearable. Including the prospect of my marriage."

"Oh? How so?"

"Because the balance between Mykola and myself was broken. And therefore had to be restored."

"Ah, to square accounts." At last he grasped her meaning. Trying to project an impassive face, he must have failed, because she reached over to clasp his hand.

"Complicated, I tried to warn you." She kissed his palm, then placed it on her cheek.

"Would it simplify matters were your husband, say, out of the picture?"

Immediately he regretted the joke. She looked at him, her eyes flickering with something he had seen on the faces of other women, but never before on hers, namely fear.

The following day, 12 more protesters joined the Maidan body count, and Yanukovych, unable to modify his grip on power, seemed destined to lose it. His replacement would almost certainly indulge the West's overtures at the expense of Russian honor. Just then, however, Putin faced an altogether different headache.

Those hooligan minstrels Pussy Riot had chosen that very moment to descend on Sochi and perform their latest cacophony, "Putin Will Teach You to Love the Motherland."

Their public whipping, by incensed Cossacks, had gone viral — the girls could not have planned it any better — and now his deputies argued which side to prosecute. Boxed into a corner, Putin ordered an inquest, then changed his mind and, though it was unlike him, put off making a decision. He tabled the meeting and left, still fuming about Pussy Riot, their garish neon balaclavas. How stupid to have freed them, right before the Olympics, since no one gave him credit. He should have let them rot.

Back in the private quarters, he found Sonia listening to his shortwave radio, a broadcast about Maidan. Noticing him in the doorway, she shut it off.

"You are allowed to use my things, Sonia," he said, irritated by the show of servility.

"So many people," she murmured. "Is there really nothing you can do?"

She squinted at him, seedlings of fear since grown from the day before, and he berated himself for having planted them. Taking her hand, he led her to the bed, determined to repair the damage. "Sonia Ivanovna," he said, cradling her chin and running his thumb along her chapped lower lip. "I've just gotten off the phone with Viktor Fedorovych."

"Really? You spoke to President Yanukovych?"

"Demanding an end to the violence."

How her eyes sparkled! As though he had given her the world's largest diamond, only better. She began pulling at his clothes and smothering him with kisses. Before long, she'd climbed on top and was grinding against him. Never had she given herself with such abandon, painting him with sweat, and for the first time, she allowed herself to be gratified. It thrilled him to feel her thighs shudder against his ribs, beyond all self-control, and the moment she pressed her lips against his ear and whispered, "Volodya," he dissolved into helpless shivers of his own.

"But how can you love him," he asked, the moment he'd caught his breath, "when you call your marriage a prison?"

Startled, she blinked. "Because I do love him," she said, "that's my prison."

Maybe he should have let her revelation stand for what it was, an intimacy freely given, though a gift Putin didn't want. Instead, he said, "Let me take care of you."

"Even if I summoned the will to divorce," she said, "how are you and I to find balance together, what with your agents watching every postcard I write?"

Balance, again, her relentless measure. With his return to Moscow just days away, he should be disengaging from her, not arguing, in the clumsiest language possible, that love surely created its own balance. At this point, her eyes grew moist, with pity, he assumed, as though she'd been debating with a pimply adolescent, unschooled in the realpolitik of emotion, when suddenly she confessed, "Of course, I have feelings for you. Of course I do," she repeated, as though in response to the look of surprise on his face. "And in another time and place, who knows? Our world could be different."

Putin remained quiet, elated to have won such a meaningful concession and afraid to add anything that might curse it. Once again she fell asleep in his arms, and much as he wished to lie like that with her indefinitely, he'd left a great deal of work undone.

Stealing away, he would not see her again till the next afternoon.

Then, while presided over a meeting — his advisers still arguing over Pussy Riot — he saw, past the guard now opening the conference room door, Sonia Ivanovna standing on tiptoe.

"Excuse me a moment, gentlemen," he said, rising from the table. In the hallway, he asked, "What is it, Sonia?"

"I thought you spoke to Yanukovych." Apparently she'd been listening once again to the shortwave.

"Sonia, this will have to wait."

"Another 50!" Her bloodshot eyes seemed to accuse him of complicity, at the very least indifference. "Innocent people are dying!"

Which, he wondered, was the less damning admission one could make to a lover? That one's power sometimes led to terrible events, or that it had its limits? Remembering the watchful eyes of his staff, he snapped, "If they're so innocent, why aren't they home with their families?"

That last word, *families*, seemed to strike her with the same force as if he'd used his hand.

"Madame is not well," he explained to the nearby guard. "Escort her back to the private quarters."

"No, I wish to go home," she said, being led away.

"Please get some rest, Sonia." Putin turned to his aide. "She is to have absolute peace and quiet. Until I return, understood?"

"Yes, Mr. President."

"And make sure the dog gets walked."

—

Barely pausing to eat, he immersed himself in work. Yanukovych, soon banished by his own parliament, needed asylum, which Putin felt duty-bound to grant. The fleet at Sevastopol also required his attention, so too the many ethnic Russians stranded beyond the national embrace. After the games — by a matter of hours, probably — he should go ahead and repatriate Crimea. Were the operation executed carefully enough, he foresaw the entire peninsula reabsorbed without a single shot.

He longed in that moment to go reassure Sonia, this time in all sincerity. Did any part of her still have feelings for him, he wondered, and what would it resemble, this life of so-called "balance," in which he'd be expected to answer for every little thing? The idea threatened something deep within his person, and not just as head of state, but why would *anyone*, even the lowliest ragpicker, yield control to another if he didn't absolutely have to? In the final analysis, it seemed unfathomable. And yet, he thought, recalling her touch, what if?

Mr. President, sir. His aide startled him from the doorway. *Sorry to interrupt.*

Putin glared at his desk. "What is so important?"

Mr. President needs to ready himself for the closing ceremonies, sir.

Ah yes, he'd almost forgotten. As he neared the private quarters, he hoped, now that Kiev had finally managed to calm itself, so had Sonia. He asked the posted guard, "How is she?"

"Sleeping, Mr. President."

In the anteroom he passed her luggage, all packed and ready, then entered the bedchamber, nearly tripping over the dog's ball. The air smelled stale, suggesting he'd been away much longer than he'd thought. Sonia's chest rose and fell, with the innocent breath of slumber, beneath the flag of his pajama top. *What if*, he wondered, *what if?*

Leaning over, Putin blew against her cheek. Her lashes fluttered, but her eyes remained shut. In a whisper, he promoted the closing ceremonies, and expressed the hope she might join him. "There'll be another fireworks show, with a wonderful joke about the fifth Olympic ring," he promised. "Once again, it will seem to fail. Then, at the last possible moment, just as the world assumes the worst of us, dear Sonia, this time the ring will bloom."

But she continued to sleep, or pretend, absolute in her silence. Maxim, on the other hand, whimpered by his feet with excitement. Reaching for the Super-Ball, Putin lobbed it across his suite and watched the little dog give chase then return it to his hand, licking his fingers with such instinctual affection one could only marvel at its purity. Putin threw the ball again, shattering a candy dish, and once more, this time a lamp. Her eyes still closed, Sonia seemed to flinch, but the dog could not be happier.

Mr. President, said his aide, *the closing ceremonies.*

"Of course," conceded Putin, then threw the ball a little harder. "Soon."

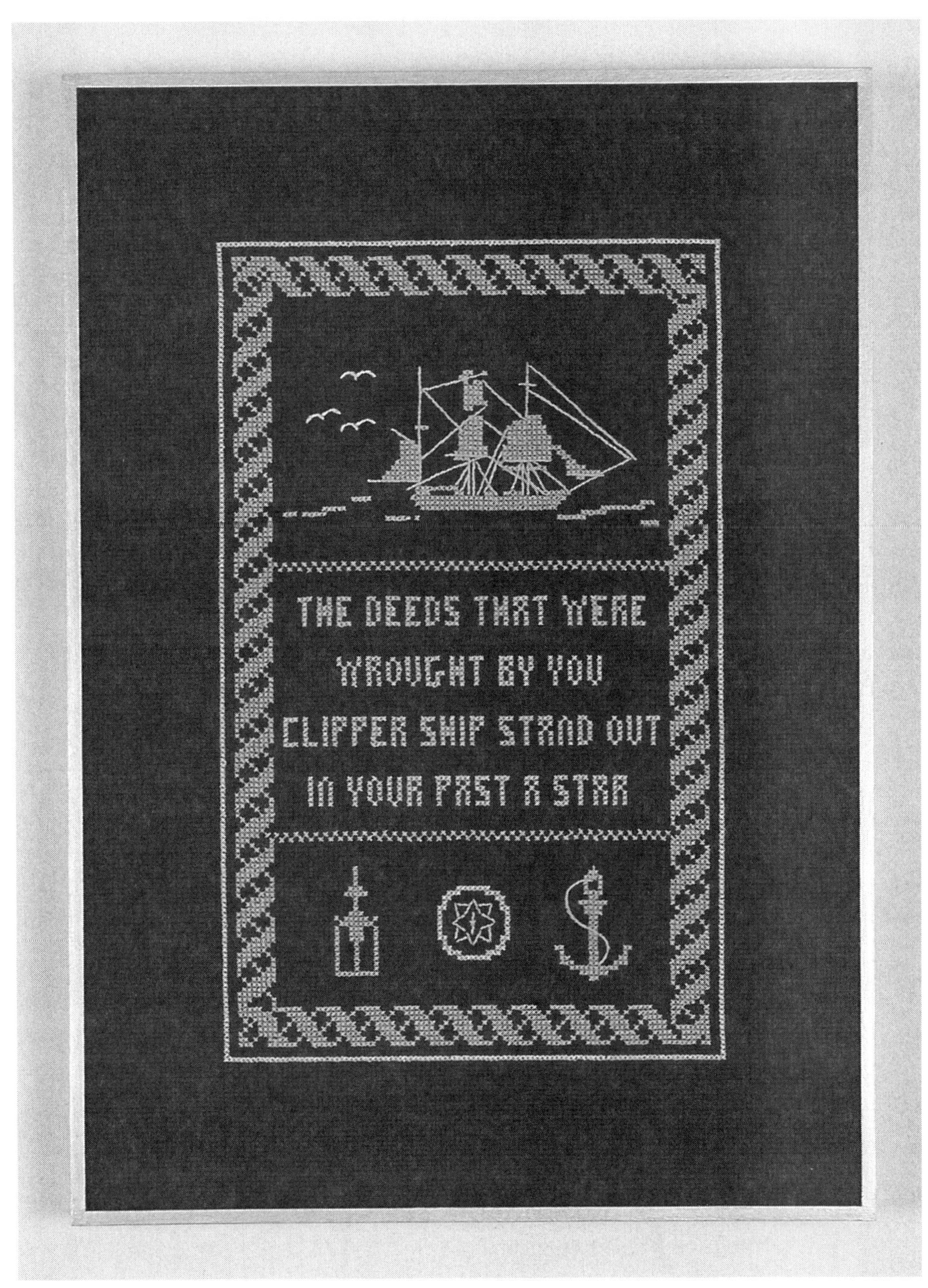

ANISSA MACK
VOYAGE OF THE CLIPPER SHIP, 2009
CROSS STITCH, ARTIST'S FRAME; 16 X 11"
COURTESY OF THE ARTIST AND LAUREL GITLEN, NEW YORK

It's Getting Hot in Here so Take Off All Your Clothes

MORGAN PARKER

All day men shout like lizards, sharp-tongued
in the desert for salty flies. The sky's the boss
of us: I can't spit when I try. In the heat, less
is everything: respect, power, mouths, sex.
All of it is taken from me. I step into a volcano
& melt like the witch I am. I want to be flawed

all the way to bed. Wake up, flawless.
Subjected, flawless. Swallowed my tongue
for communion. I mean, volcano.
I erupt with a mouth like a bossy
eagle. I made my bed so I have sex
in it. My body gets more for less

& O! When I say less
I mean as in classically beautiful, flaws
spilling out of my mouth like sexy
moon rocks. I cut out men's tongues &
I sharpen myself & I'm scary & I'm bossy:
I'm the chick who raises snakes like a volcano

spews its desert under pressure. Volcanic
in the streets & volcanic in the bed. Less
kitchenware, more potent libidos bossing
men around. All day they shout, flaws
on my crystal. All day I feel their tongues.
It's literal, it isn't sexual.

Okay maybe it is about sex.
What passes for magic. How a sleeping volcano
is still a volcano. How with my tongue
I turn on a light like god & I have less
privilege than god. How even with flaws
under these clothes I could be the boss

of you without them. Magic. Boss
you all night long. & of course I mean sex
but I mean teaching, too. Black girl rage, flawless.
This diamond my diamond in a volcano's
hot, lost city. & I do not mean helpless.

< SIMONE FORTI
SONG OF THE VOWELS, 2009
GRAPHITE AND MARKER ON PAPER, 26 5/8 X 21 1/8"
COURTESY OF THE ARTIST AND THE BOX, LA

ALL GOOD SCIENCE FICTION BEGINS THIS WAY

INGRID ROJAS CONTRERAS

We don't want to conquer space at all.
We want to expand earth endlessly.
We don't want other worlds; we want a mirror.
Solaris, Stanisław Lem

THREE DAYS BEFORE the wedding, when I was riding my bike to pick up my wedding dress, a car door opened in front of me. The thing I most recall about the accident is not the moment of impact but just after. How I imagine my brain — coiled and white — pitching forward in fluid. How I sit up and hold my head as if to stop my brain from hitting the cranium. How when I break my eyes open, there is a man in glasses next to me pulling me to my feet. He is the same man who flung his car door in front of me causing me to crash, so I brush his hands away and say, *I am fine, I am going to ride away now.* I straddle my seat and push my feet on the pedals but the wheels do not move. The man lurches up to me. He avoids my eyes. He pins the front wheel between his knees. He yanks the crooked handlebar back into place.

Next, I am a reveler, walking along the city sidewalk, trailing my bike behind me as people in business suits and winter hats brush past me inflamed with purpose. Then I stand still at the corner, mesmerized by the street signs — *Madison*, *Halsted* — because not only do I *not* recognize the names, it suddenly dawns on me: I have no idea where I came from or where I was going, what city I am in, what my name is, and I do not even know the year.

Somewhere, *somehow*, this strikes me as funny. Nay, *hilarious*. Am I laughing out loud? I half-reach to stop someone to ask them the year, and if they don't freak out maybe the city, but I pull back in a giggle, knowing *this is life imitating, life imitating …*

And it is at this crucial moment when the man who flung his door at me passes me whistling in his coat and hat, walking a small white poodle. Then a sentence pops into my head, the way words sometimes do, of their own volition, just pop into your mind: *All good science fiction begins this way.*

It's a story where … It's on the tip of my tongue. But it's hard to focus because I am raging with electricity. I am air packed together in sheer consciousness. I close my eyes. I give in to the current.

I exult in the corner. There is the noise of traffic, the bustling of people. I am euphoria standing in place.

When I open my eyes, how much time has passed? All appears to be the same: people waiting, then crossing at the red light. Cars going, cars idling. *I am so, I feel so,* there is nothing to do but wait for this wave of devotion to pass. *Devotion to what?* I close my eyes. *I am so, I feel so.*

How long did you lose your memory for? people ask when I tell this story, but the answer is never straightforward. My memory loss looks like a barren rocky island shaped by an ocean that is no longer there. The horizon, once blue never-ending water, is a canyon. I trace the steep cliffs, the striations in the rocks, the slope down to the sea floor. The metronome of the beating ocean is gone. Without it, time is slow and viscous. After the accident, I immediately decide my ocean will return, so I keep my memory loss a secret. But I am also aware that I am hiding a dark desire even from myself: I never ever want to be taken away from that barren place. I like the scarcity of the black rocks, the clean feeling, the eeriness — I have so many questions I want to ask of the still-wet deserted ocean floor.

When I open my eyes, how much time has passed? I am standing on the corner of Madison and Halsted. The crowd, the cars, the red light. Everything is bright and pure and unmitigated. I feel so powerful I try to stand still, because it's the only way I know I will not explode or drift off into space like a combustive celestial body. Everything is possible, every conceivable future, when you are without a past.

But for someone as powerful as I feel, standing still is boring. I look down Halsted Street as it stretches to the horizon with small shops and condos, and I calculate possibilities, companions, adventures. *I can marry someone rich,* I think, looking down Madison at the tall, luxurious skyscrapers. *I can become a sailor.* This is better, but how do I get to shore? I am standing on my toes, ready to walk, *not a sailor* but what? *A banker,* I think, *yes, a bank teller in a pretty suit depositing people's checks into.* Then everything stops suddenly.

I see a woman through a glass storefront, and at lightning speed I understand that the glance I just gave her — noncommittal, *arrogant* — I gave to myself. I am looking at myself in the reflection of the darkened window. My hair is black and in disarray and I am holding my bike next to me like a steed. People walk around me, staring beyond me like I'm not even there, like a miracle is not just unfolding before all of our eyes — because it feels miraculous, the seeing of myself for the first time. I watch with astonishment as my own eyes (harried, unbelieving, flown open) communicate back to me every inch and ebb of how I am feeling.

I come up close to the window. I am beautiful. I examine my face — the thick eyebrows, the brown skin, the wide nose. *What heritage is written on that face — South American, Middle Eastern, Caribbean?* I have no idea. I run my finger on my brow, caress my own cheek, play with my hair. *God, my eyebrows are so thick.*

It occurs to me there might be marks on my body or clues on my clothes (an African bracelet, maybe, a pin with a flag), but there are none. *How did I know my gender all this time?* I realize I have opened a door I might not be able to close. Now I have to decide: do I call the ocean back to me or do I continue my life as a barren island?

I stand in front of the window hesitating before my reflection, weighing the awfulness of not knowing myself versus the lightness of being a blank slate. *What more science fiction than this?* I watch the cycle of the red light. *Go, Slow, Stop.*

Islands can often seem like a floating slice of land, but beneath the water surface, tall escarpments take root and run aground. Most oceanic islands are volcanic. All across the Pacific, volcanoes rise out of the seafloor. They spew out ash and cinders and iridescent lava that solidifies into layer after layer of growing domes. During the making of an island, great explosions of water and sand shoot out into the air. Lava pours out and cools almost immediately. Serene white plumes of sulfur and steam braid into the sky, and the volcano breaks the surface of the water. Oceanic islands are born of fire.

A woman on the phone who identifies herself as my sister informs me I am getting married in three days. Because I have no sense of time in the wake of the accident, I keep time to the metronome of others. I dance to the punctuations of what I think is expected of me. When the man she tells me is my fiancé strips that first night and lies naked in bed, I understand I must do the same.

I don't care how far I have to go to keep my amnesia a secret. I love its strange vibration, and I don't want anyone to fix it. I am at every moment soaring. I don't care that I am lost to my past since I am absolutely found to myself. An island in the ocean, the ocean gone away.

I drop my clothes. I get in bed. My fiancé presses his chest up to my back. He drapes his arm over my stomach. Then his body relaxes.

You don't want sex? I ask.

No, I want to hold you.

My fiancé has to wake me up every hour to make sure my brain is not swelling. He is supposed to ask me simple questions, like *What is one plus one?* That's the doctor's example in the emergency room as he checks a box on a form. At night, in bed, I feel like a game-show contestant. I know I have to study my answers, but it's hard to stay afloat, *one plus one is two, his name is Jeremiah, my name is Ingrid, the city is Chicago, the year is 2007. No, 2008. No, 2007.* I fall asleep so easily I don't even notice I have fallen asleep.

My shoulder shakes. I hear Jeremiah's voice: *What is your name?* It is dark in my apartment *or are we in my apartment?* If I answer correctly I can go back to sleep again. *Ingrid*, I say. Something is wrong, but I can't remember what. Sleep is white fuzz. It wants me so badly. But I have to stay awake. I fight the marshmallow of nothingness, but soon I am consumed in it.

Jeremiah is shaking me again, *Where are you from?* Nobody told me this question would be on the test. *Leave me alone*, I huff. *I'm sleepy. Just tell me where you're from*, he insists. Suddenly I remember what's troubling me. It's the million-dollar question: *Who am I sleeping next to?* I feel unsafe. *I'm from*

Colombia, I answer. I remind myself I am pretending I haven't lost my memory. I snuggle my back to him — his body strange and unfamiliar.

An island in the ocean, the ocean gone away.

I dream that Jeremiah is my brother, even though I seem to know I don't have a brother in real life. Maybe I give him that identity because I'm not sure who he is. Or maybe, as a psychoanalyst explains years later, I invent this sibling relationship so that in my moment of trauma I can experience a more innocent facet of love. But it doesn't work out that way. Instead I dream I am naked in his bed. Do I dream he is confronting me, that he himself is telling me we are related in this way? It feels like only a second has passed and Jeremiah is shaking me again, *Tell me what my name is.*

In the years that follow, this will happen again: 12 times that first year, eight the second, and now on random occasions that seem like aftershocks.

Late at night when I am in that space between dreaming and waking, I believe that Jeremiah is my brother. I sit up and cling to the bedsheet and move away because I am naked and he is too. I cover my face. I try to perceive whether there is semen. I try hard to remember an instance of a condom, a pill, a sponge.

Sometimes there is semen. Sometimes there is no semen.

I cringe at what our mother will think.
Then I realize I cannot bring her to mind.
That's when a thought comes gurgling as if through water —
I've done this before.
Even the gestures, I realize, are replicas of other nights.

Oceanic islands are an assembly of igneous rock — red rhyolite, black basalt, pale and porous pumice. Then the ocean brings life: mussels, shellfish, and coral. Shells and dead corals wash ashore and are ground down into sand. Birds come to rest their wings and leave seeds behind in their droppings. Shrubs and ferns sprout up.

And if the ocean were to retreat?

You would be able to look down the cliff of the great volcanic cone. You would be able to climb down the crisp, hardened mounds, and see the black wrinkles on the rock face. You could reconstruct the story of how and where the lava erupted, how it traveled, how the island formed. You could come close to the central vent where all the lava came from.

I stand in front of the window at Madison and Halsted hesitating before my reflection, weighing the awfulness of not knowing myself versus the lightness of being a blank slate. I try to break into the fortress of my mind by staring into my iris. It occurs to me I could be an illegal immigrant. *I have to avoid the authorities.* I search up and down the street for cops. *I could be one of the millions undocumented, working for low wages, desperate, prone to predation. Prone to predation?* I ask myself. Even then this strikes me as an odd sentence construction.

I take a breath. I pull on the bag strap that's been digging into my shoulder and consider the purse, white and worn, with little printed stars. *I can look in my bag and find out who I am.* I pull my bike to the intersection, satisfied with this decision. I cross the street. *I'll just see what my name is, then I'll put the bag in a trash can.* I stop by a chain-link fence and sit down, pulling everything out and spreading it before me on the pavement.

A journal, a wallet, keys, a novel, a cell phone. I open the wallet and take out an Illinois ID card. I am staring at myself again. I look so carefree. I am wearing blue eye shadow and thick liner. I read my name over and over again without its becoming familiar. This desire for familiarity is unexpected. *If only I can see how others see me, then I will know who I am.* I open the journal. I fan the pages before my eyes, but I don't recognize the handwriting. I am patient and serene. Then, like turning a corner, I am terrified. I am choking. *Am I having a panic attack?* I do not care that I'm a public spectacle. I am screaming. *Am I having a breakdown?* Out of the corner of my eye I see people are crossing the streets on all intersections to avoid me.

MEDICAL INSTRUCTIONS

Post-concussion syndrome often follows a mild head injury. Dizziness, mild nausea, mild headache, trouble concentrating, and a general sense of "not being right" may persist for a week or two.

Jeremiah is reading, but I am thinking about the previous night in the emergency room. In the little curtained-off space the doctor shines a light into my eyes. He takes an x-ray of my brain. He avoids the word *amnesia*, but everything he asks seems a dance around the word: *Are you having trouble remembering anything? Is anything strange?* I tango in response. *No, everything is normal.* I turn to Jeremiah. *Right?* Jeremiah nods. He looks distressed. I am sure I would feel sympathy for him if I remembered him, but I don't. The doctor studies my every move and word. I smile, glance at his pen poised over my paperwork, and stare directly into his eyes.

While vigorous exercise may worsen the headache, mild physical activity often is helpful. Sitting and thinking about your symptoms will worsen them.

Jeremiah lays some pills for me on a little tray. It's two days to the wedding and in order to buy myself time so I can study my mind, I have to play the part of his fiancée. I stretch my back like a cat, and as he's smiling, I ask him to write me a to-do list so I can keep track of what wedding tasks are left.

But I have to get to work. He looks at his watch. *Anyway, everything's done. We don't need a list.*

But I feel like we're forgetting something — can't you humor me?

I learn that we have planned two wedding ceremonies: one for his conservative parents in October, and one for my liberal parents come May. There isn't much to prepare for the October ceremony. Jeremiah tells me we will get married with six people present, dinner out, dancing, a night away. It's specifically pared down so that we can have a wild, hippie wedding later on. My only responsibility before Saturday is to pick up the wedding dress. I tell him I will go today, but once alone I don't move. There's a weird bamboo bookshelf, used orange furniture, silky ribbons hanging by the windows, and the kitchen is jam-packed with utensils and spoons and pots piled on shelves piled on *other* shelves. There are so many plants I feel like I am in a jungle, and there are three cats constantly mewing at me, batting at my heels wherever I go. I don't recognize anything.

My mother and father call me on my cell phone. They speak to me in Spanish. I am surprised I understand, but more so at the sound of their voices — how *familiar* they are, how much like a door left open just a crack.

Me estás escuchando, Ingrid Carolina? My mother is calling to beg me not to wear the black dress to my wedding.

The black dress. I marvel at the fact that even though I cannot recall my family or my fiancé, I can still picture the dress. It's a silk Vera Wang with a plunging neckline, an empire waist, and a long train. The bodice and the shoulders are my favorite parts — the folds of black silk covering the breasts, the rosettes gathering at the waist, the silk ruffling and curling just barely at the shoulder. This is the dress my mother is arguing will trigger events to make me a young widow. *You and your feminist concepts. Listen to me — no seas terca.*

Am I stubborn? I wonder. *Is losing your memory like being widowed?* I *was* on my way to pick up the dress when the accident happened. I push the thought away. I have been quiet for one second too many. I can't remember what kind of rapport I have with my mother, but I plow ahead. *No, I am sure. I am wearing the black dress.*

The idea of telling my mother what's happened doesn't occur to me. And all the seconds I am quiet, withholding information, I am aware that I am not doing it out of shame, but because *I don't want her to have the satisfaction of being right.*

It's just a dress, I add. *Stop trying to jinx it with superstition.*

I hang up. I go to the dining table, itching with excitement, eager to poke at my mind to see how many layers I can peel back. Does the mind have a center? If it does, I want to arrive there. I sit down. *Who are you now that everything has been stripped bare?* But my mind is quiet. *What are you now that you have no identity?* But my mind is solid and aloof and quite remote to myself.

When you are blind with desire, you do not care about consequences. Curiosity can be a violent force hurling you to new shores, but at what price? I wonder now about Pliny the Elder, who after the eruption of Mount Vesuvius got on a ship — not to help with the evacuation but to selfishly observe the violent spectacle. His deckhands advised him to turn back, but he was firm: "Fortune favors the bold." He disembarked amidst a rain of cinders and pumice a few miles from the volcano only to die some hours later, probably from the toxic fumes. Pliny. His fate was irrepressibly tied to volcanoes. He wrote of the birth and death of islands, like the one that emerged in his lifetime in the Aegean Sea. During the celebration of the eighth centennial of the founding of Rome, between five and nine in the evening, during a total moon eclipse, a mile-wide piece of burning land surfaced. The Greeks named the island *Thia*, the Godly. Poseidon, god of the oceans, was believed to be behind such creations. It must have been a spectacular sight, but not a surprising one: this location had been producing and dissolving islands for centuries. The geographer Strabo wrote of Thia's sister island Hiera: "flames rose out of the waves for four days, so that the whole sea boiled and blazed, and they gradually threw up an island."

⁓

How long have I been screaming? I am not sure, but my voice is hoarse. I look at the contents of my purse, wondering how I will walk away. Then I see an Asian man approaching. He is striking to me because he is old, has a bad foot, and leans on a cane. When he stops before me, I see his cane is a tree branch covered in lacquer. I witness his effort as he bends down. I see the way his mottled, wrinkled hands with knobby fingers roam around his pocket and then he's extending a 20-dollar bill to me.

I don't take it, so he lifts my journal. *Is he trying to buy my writing? Buy my story?* But he only places the bill on the pavement and my journal on top as a paperweight. His hands, long-fingered and with knots at the joints, come together at his chest and he bows — two, three times — like I am a goddess. *A goddess of what?* He rises slowly and walks backward a few steps, still facing me, like time itself is going back and back. He turns. He crosses the street. He is gone.

⁓

At the emergency room I sit in a curtained-off space and wait for the doctor to return. The doctor has left my curtain open so I see the man whose singing I have been hearing all along. He is wearing a flowery white hospital robe with a slit in the back and nothing else except black ankle socks. He is about 40, gliding along the hall, singing. Then he comes close and recites his poetry to me. I watch his body sway, the way his feet come up just a bit off the tile as he raps out words that I drink and drink. And just as I am becoming aware that *I love this right now*, that *I love this man right now*, he breaks off his recitation. "You're a writer," and I am so taken aback by his statement, I worry that my memory is lapsing again. "Did *I* tell you that?"

"No, man, I just know."

⁓

If I have coffee I can be awake enough to think of more questions to ask myself. I crawl to the kitchen. I stand before the espresso machine. It has silver accents and bulky knobs. I try to decode the curious hieroglyphs, *cup with waves*, *mushroom cloud*, *smaller cup*. I drink water and sleep. Each time I nap and wake up I remember more things, except they are small — the image of a steaming cup of soup in my hands, the silhouette of somebody in a bar throwing their head back in laughter. I am by the hour more flesh and blood. I decide I have to figure out how to pick up the dress, then I can study my mind, but I've only advanced a few steps when I see my journals on the bookshelf and realize I am marrying a man I cannot remember and what I need to do is get more backstory. I pull down all the journals and read the oldest one, looking for clues. *Is Jeremiah the right man to marry? Am I the marrying type? Why am I getting married?*

I know journals are supposed to be a bear-all account, but the writing is vague. One page reads, "I have gone to bed with an empty heart for three nights in a row. I feel that air fails me." The rest of the page is blank.

Another page: "Cramping a blanket, nails digging."

There are strange lists:

Memories of What the Sky Looks Like from the Backseat of a Moving Car

Ways in Which Pets Have Died

And there are pages filled with overheard conversations.

In the whole book, I only find one entry that could be about my fiancé:

My head against his chest. The resonating heart, the echoing voice, and the muscles tensing up periodically as he flips a page of Hemingway. Hemingway settling into the carpeted floor and his crumpled sheets. I twirl my fingers in the waist of his shirt. The words transcend my brain in images.

I lower the journal and wait for the memory that is lapping up. I see a small room, a gray carpet, a too-small bed, the small black hole of his belly button. I don't want the ocean to return. I feel the heft of those few details like manifest weight on my shoulders. I leave the journals as they are. I can't keep reading. My eyes are already closing before I can get to the bedroom.

If the earth were to speak, volcanoes would be the mouthpiece. The things that erupt from volcanoes come from the earth's center, but because of the volatility and pressure, scientists can only theorize about what dwells there. They believe mostly iron, because it's the heaviest mineral, and it's what would sift down to the center. We know that beneath the crust of the earth there's a layer of magma. Beneath that, it is believed there is a sea of swirling iron encircling a solid ball of iron that is so hot and pressurized, it is rotating slowly.

I realize I can find my family by looking in my phone for the last name I found on my ID, but when I pick up the cell phone I remember a face and then a name. I see the high golden forehead, the green-blue eyes. His name is Jeremiah and he is someone I care about, but I don't know *who. Who is Jeremiah?* I search around the half-remembered image of his face. He's the only person I can call for help, but I don't call him. I don't know what our relationship is, and I need to know so I can act my part well. I call the last person I spoke to — GEOFF S. Who is he? I don't know. But maybe he can clarify who Jeremiah is. I don't know how I will ask this question without giving myself away, but I am already dialing, checking the name on my phone screen, and the clicking sound of someone answering comes on and I am speaking. *Hi Geoff, how are you?* To my own ears I sound put together.

INGRID? What's wrong? Where are you? Are you okay? Where are you?

I don't remember what I say, only that I am crying again. I hold my head and try to control my breathing as Geoff lists the details of my life — that I have a sister, that my sister is his fiancée, that I am in Chicago, that Jeremiah is *my* fiancé, that I've been dating Jeremiah for five years, that I need to get to a hospital, that everything will be okay.

It's the adrenaline, I say. *It's making it hard to think straight.*

Geoff says he understands. He doesn't seem suspicious and makes me swear I will call Jeremiah, but after we hang up I am freaking out. *How will I mask this? How will I cover it up?* I hold my breath. I swallow everything down. I am dialing Jeremiah now, I am planning what to say, *Hi, Jeremiah, how are you? I had a little accident, could you come help?* By Jeremiah's hysterical response I realize I am not actually speaking out loud, just crying and blubbering two phrases — "I fell" and "I don't remember" — while he asks me two questions: "What happened? Where are you?"

Eventually I walk to the corner and read the street signs, but when we hang up I graduate to a new level of panic. I try to speed-read through the journal I found, but I can't. I cannot deal with not having control, and the panic I feel grows in a converse relationship to my loss of control. The words blur and come together in my vision.

—~—

In the wake of the accident, I spend a lot of time lying down, staring at my mind. It's entertaining being such a void. I don't think about anything. My mind is a quiet island. My mind will not answer any of my questions. It buzzes instead with an uncanny beauty. The landscape is desolate, and white seagulls every now and then dive down. I am swooped along onto plateau after plateau of the unnameable.

Jeremiah calls on my cell phone. *I have to work late. Did you pick up your dress?* I tell him I will. Then we hang up.

I daydream about my options: I could walk. I could take a bus. But the dress is expensive. *What if someone tries to steal it?* There's no way I am biking again. I can only call a taxi. But which service is the best? The receipt for the dress is in my purse: *The Dress Doctor, Since 1982.* As soon as I see it, I recall the face of the seamstress. Actually what I remember is her hair. It's silver and short and beautifully curled. I remember how she asked, *Why* ever *did you choose black?* I remember the luxury of the fitting room, the elegant feeling of going in and stepping onto the cream-colored platform in my underwear, suddenly flanked by three images of myself. Tall curtains rose up behind me, royal red and velvet, heavy with long golden cords. I remember hearing the woman in the adjacent stall detailing the changes she wanted made.

I don't have enough memories yet, so I make a parallel to the emergency room — how the space at the hospital was also not a room but a curtained-off space. The curtains at the emergency room were blue (or maybe white) and thin. I listened in on the people around me there as well. Behind me, someone whispered in what sounded like German, far off there was laughter, and farther still one person was shrieking.

—~—

It's a new morning and when I decide to move around, to eat something, to wash dishes, to feed the mewing cats, a feeling comes over me. It's like a terrible omen. I tense up in place, waiting. Then a high-pitched terror with no words attached breaks the surface. I hang onto a wall. It feels like I am about to lose my mind. I try to breathe. I want to know what is happening to me, but when I move to untangle the emotion, the high-pitched terror subsumes. Like forgetting a name or forgetting a face, the texture and the shape of the terrible thing just disappears. That's the first appearance of it, the high-pitched terror, but it comes and goes every other hour. I don't think I will be able to pick up the dress, but I have no choice. I am quick and quiet. I hold on to my temples in the taxi, ask him to wait, then I hug the dress all the way home. It is late when I return, but I hang the dress on a padded hanger. *It's so pretty. See?* I run my fingers through the fine black silk. *My mother is crazy. There's nothing supernatural about this dress.* I lift the train. I fluff it. I let it fall. I kick all my clothes off and put it on. I prance around in my apartment. I water the plants, I sashay to the windows. I let the train slide on the floor even though I know it's dirty and the cats may attack.

The best thing to do when the high-pitched terror breaks the surface is to breathe. To just space out for a while, go into that sheltered space where I can wait out any storm. Not exactly step out of myself, more like watch myself as a specimen. Watch suffering as an alien affliction. Stand in awe of the terrible: *What more science fiction than this?*

Volcanoes erupt because eventually the core of the earth has to shed off its heat. Its hot currents upset through the liquid iron and boil into magma, and then rivers of lava break through the crust and run aglow. One more thing about the island that emerged in Pliny the Elder's time:

It sank back into the earth's crust, and now in its stead, there are two new islands, the Kameni islands. Yet buried within them are the others — Thia, the Godly, Hiera, the Holy, and an even more ancient, nameless island that some believe to be Atlantis. Islands fold in islands, histories into myths.

When the naturalist Edward Forbes visited the Kameni Islands in 1841, the inhabitants told him something was always happening below the surface. "Subterranean noises are not unfrequently heard, especially during calms and south winds, when, they say, the water of parts of the bay becomes the colour of sulphur."

When Jeremiah arrives he throws his bicycle on the ground and I hurl myself in his arms so he cannot see me cry. He is stroking my hair. *Shh, shh, it's all going to be okay.* We are standing in the middle of the street, and the world is whirling around us. I am lost to the world, but my head finds a nook just under his shoulder. It is a perfect nook. The feeling of my head fitting into this nook makes me still and breathless and I realize that my body remembers him. It's because of that feeling that I get in a taxi with him and hold his hand and look out the window, waiting for my ocean to return. On my wedding day I am a bruised bride with enough partial memory to act the part well. My brain is still sloshing and slow, black silk hiding the bruises on my body and trailing behind me on the floor.

It turns out that deep within the folds of the brain — at the center of my mind — there lies an expanse of wrinkled tissue called the Island of Reil, after the German physician Johann Reil. Colloquially known as the insula, the Island of Reil is where emotional life is believed to reside. It reads the state of the body and houses conscious and unconscious desires, giving a feeling or impression of what is real, true, and important.

Waking up into the amnesia of the accident, it is always the gestures (the sitting up, the closing of my eyes, the light holding of the forehead) that trigger the feeling of theater. I am an actor in a play I wrote for myself in a dream.

Then right on cue, after scrambling to remember whether we've used protection, it's the question — *Who is our shared mother?* — that makes the real memories rush back. I remember the accident, the not-recognizing my apartment. And then in a series of superimposed images, across the eight years of my marriage to Jeremiah, I see myself sitting up in bed night after night after night after night *remembering myself* sitting up in bed night after night after night after night.

Each time the realization that I keep performing the same scene from an invented memory crushes me anew.

I look down at Jeremiah, whom just moments ago I regarded in panic and disgust, and consider how soft he is in sleep. I burrow close. I think of the barren island of my mind. *What more science fiction than this?*

ANISSA MACK >
OVERLAY (OLDEST LIVING MEMORY), 2012
PAINTED AQUA RESIN, PAPER; 103 X 86 X 1/2"
COURTESY OF THE ARTIST AND LAUREL GITLEN, NEW YORK

WHITNEY HUBBS
UNTITLED, FROM THE ONGOING SERIES, *MY OWN METAPHORS*, 2015
SILVER GELATIN PRINT, 20 X 16"
COURTESY OF THE ARTIST AND M+B GALLERY, LOS ANGELES

Lemon SVEN BIRKERTS

IT WAS THE SUMMER of 1966 and the Rolling Stones's "Paint It Black" was just out. I remember because I was with my family in London and that sitar sound was snaking out of every storefront, but also because at one point my father, who always mocked my music and bands, said, "I like that song." I was 15, my sister was 12, and the four of us were on a family trip. After starting in London, we continued on to Germany, where we picked up a VW Bug that we would later ship back to the US; we then drove down through Germany and over the Swiss mountains into Italy. I was miserable the whole time. Not for me the visit to Mad Ludwig's castle looming high over its valley, or our endless tour around the town of Nördlingen, where my parents had met after the war. I hung back at every point, sulked, made my mood very clear. My sister sat with me in the back seat of the car reading a book called *Dragonwyck* — until one day my father turned and snatched it from her and — unthinkable — threw it out the window, shouting, "Look at what's around you!" I was now more determined than ever to *not* enjoy: not the outdoor summer meals where the little bees hovered over the sausages on our plates, nor the drama of going over the Gotthard Pass, nor later the vistas my parents kept pointing at as we drove slowly down into Italy. I thought only of my friends at home, all together playing pool and games of Hearts. I followed with great resistance through Verona, refusing to take in the old streets and towers, stayed silent when my mother or father would say, "Isn't this beautiful!" If I sometimes gave a nod it was only to avoid another scene — my father suddenly stopping me in the street to correct my posture, or to hiss at me about my attitude. I drew my private world close around me, made a shield that nothing could penetrate, not the slightest good thing. Except one. We had arrived in Florence, where it was unbearably hot, everything — the rooms, the streets. The four of us made our way through the blaze of the afternoon, from one famous old building to another. Finally, though, it was time for dinner. My parents found a restaurant called Sabatini and I thought of the writer who wrote *Captain Blood*. I forget now what I ate, or what we talked about, or what was around us. I only know I was parched and my legs were very tired and that after my meal I ordered Sabatini's special dessert. I do remember the waiter bringing it over — the biggest lemon I had ever seen, carved out and packed shiny with lemon "ice." I'd never tasted anything so fresh and delicious. The tang of it stayed with me, and it would be many years before I learned how time can slowly turn such pleasures inside out.

CONTRIBUTORS

KANNAN MAHADEVAN was born in Basel, Switzerland, and grew up in Prince George's County, Maryland. He is a graduate of the University of Chicago and the Iowa Writers' Workshop, where he was a Dean's Graduate Fellow and received an MFA in fiction. This is his second story to appear in the *LARB Quarterly Journal*. He is currently at work on a novel.

KAREN E. BENDER is the author of the story collection *Refund*, which is a finalist for the National Book Award, and shortlisted for the Frank O'Connor International Short Story Award; she is also the author of the novels *Like Normal People* and *A Town of Empty Rooms*.

ELLEN COLLETT is an LA–based writer with an MFA from the Bennington Writing Seminars who truthfully likes animals.

NATHALIE HANDAL's recent books include the flash collection *The Republics*, which Patricia Smith lauds as "one of the most inventive books by one of today's most diverse writers"; *The Invisible Star*, the critically acclaimed *Poet in Andalucía*; and *Love and Strange Horses*, winner of the Gold Medal Independent Publisher Book Award, which *The New York Times* says is "a book that trembles with belonging (and longing)." Handal is a Lannan Foundation Fellow, winner of the Alejo Zuloaga Order in Literature, and Honored Finalist for the Gift of Freedom Award, among other honors. She is a professor at Columbia University and writes the literary travel column The City and the Writer for *Words without Borders*.

DIONISIA MORALES lives and writes in Oregon's Willamette Valley. Her essays have appeared or are forthcoming in *Crab Orchard Review*, *Hunger Mountain*, *Colorado Review*, *Brevity*, *Oregon Humanities* magazine, and other journals.

JEREMY N. SMITH has written for *Discover*, *The Atlantic*, and *The New York Times*, among many other publications. His first book, *Growing a Garden City*, was one of *Booklist*'s top 10 books on the environment for 2011. Born and raised in Evanston, Illinois, he is a graduate of Harvard College and the University of Montana. He lives in Missoula, Montana, with his wife and young daughter. His most recent book is *Epic Measures: One Doctor. Seven Billion Patients* (HarperCollins).

JOHN RECHY is an American writer whose novels include the now classic *City of Night* and 15 other works of fiction and nonfiction. His books have been translated worldwide. He is the recipient of PEN Center USA's Lifetime Achievement Award, the Publishing Triangle's Bill Whitehead Award for Lifetime Achievement, and the Luis Leal Award in Chicano literature. A pioneer in modern American literature, and in gay and Chicano literature, he has lectured on writing and other topics at Harvard, Duke, and Yale Universities, as well as at Occidental College and various campuses of the University of California. He has written plays and essays for *The Nation*, *The Los Angeles Times*, *The Washington Post*, *The Saturday Review*, *The New York Times*, *The Advocate*, *Mother Jones*, and many other publications. His forthcoming novel — "a true fiction" — is *Island! Island!*

MILJOHN RUPERTO lives and works in Los Angeles. He was born in 1971 in Manila, Philippines, and received his MFA in Sculpture from Yale University in 2002 and his BA, Studio Art from University of California, Berkeley in 1999.

RINI YUN KEAGY received her MFA in Film and Media Arts from Temple University in Philadelphia. Her moving image practice in video and 16mm film is multi-modal and research-based, and investigates race and labor, disease, and sites of historical and psychological trauma. She spent her early childhood in rural Guatemala, and has lived in the US, Cuba, France, Indonesia, and Thailand. She has taught film production and studies at the University of the Arts, UC Santa Cruz, and Carleton College.

ROBERT ANTHONY SIEGEL is the author of two novels, *All Will Be Revealed* and *All the Money in the World*. His nonfiction has appeared in *The Paris Review*, *Tin House*, *Ploughshares*, *The Oxford American*, *The New York Times*, the *Los Angeles Times*, and elsewhere. A book of essays is forthcoming from Counterpoint Press. He was a Fulbright fellow in Taiwan in 2014. His website is www.robertanthonysiegel.com.

ANGELA WOODWARD's novel *Natural Wonders* won the Fiction Collective Two Doctorow Prize for Innovative Fiction in 2015. She is also author of the novel *End of the Fire Cult* and the collections *Origins and Other Stories and The Human Mind.*

WILLA CARROLL was the winner of *Tupelo Quarterly*'s TQ7 Poetry Prize, judged by Brenda Hillman, and *Narrative Magazine*'s Third Annual Poetry Contest. She was nominated for a Pushcart Prize and placed as a semifinalist for the "Discovery" / Boston Review Contest. Her poems have appeared in *Tin House*, *Tuesday*, *An Art Project*, *Poemeleon*, *Stone Canoe*, *Structo*, *Free State Review*, and elsewhere. Video readings of her poems are online in *Narrative*.

JOSH BELL has taught in the MFA program at Columbia University and is currently Briggs-Copeland Lecturer on English at Harvard University. He is the author of *No Planets Strike* and his next book is forthcoming from Copper Canyon Press in early 2016.

REBECCA CHACE is the author of: *Leaving Rock Harbor* (novel); *Capture the Flag* (novel); *Chautauqua Summer* (Memoir). Plays: *Colette; The Awakening* (adaptation of novel by Kate Chopin). Ms. Chace adapted her novel *Capture the Flag* for the screen with director Lisanne Skyler; the Showtime Tony Cox Screenwriting Award (Short Film), Nantucket Film Festival, 2010. She has written for *The New York Times Magazine, The New York Times Sunday Book Review,* the *Huffington Post*, NPR's *All Things Considered*, and other publications. She is Director of creative writing at Fairleigh Dickinson University and 2014 recipient of the Grace Paley Fiction Fellowship at Vermont Studio Center.

She is a 2015–2016 member of the Wertheim Study at the NYPL and lives in Brooklyn.

BEN PACK lives in Los Angeles and teaches writing and critical reasoning at USC. When not discussing TV, pop music, and kids, he and his boyfriend fantasize about defying their apartment's no-pet policy in order to get a dog. They plan to adopt.

PETER GADOL's six novels include *The Long Rain*, *Light at Dusk*, and *Silver Lake*, which was nominated for awards from the Southern California Independent Bookseller Association and the Lambda Literary Foundation. His short fiction has appeared in *Tin House*, *Story*, *Bloom*, *StoryQuarterly*, and the *LARB Quarterly Journal*. The recipient of fellowships from the NEA, Yaddo, and the Djerassi Resident Artists Program, Gadol is Chair and Professor of Graduate Writing at Otis College of Art and Design.

IRA SUKRUNGRUANG is the author of the memoirs *Southside Buddhist* and *Talk Thai: the Adventures of Buddhist Boy*, and the poetry collection *In Thailand It Is Night*. He is the recipient of the 2015 American Book Award, New York Foundation for the Arts Fellowship in Nonfiction Literature, an Arts and Letters Fellowship, and the Emerging Writer Fellowship. He is one of the founding editors of *Sweet: A Literary Confection* (sweetlit.com), and teaches in the MFA program at University of South Florida. For more information about him, please visit: www.buddhistboy.com.

MAX NELSON is a New York–based film critic who regularly contributes to *Reverse Shot*, *Cinema Scope*, and *Film Comment*, where he writes a bimonthly column on new and upcoming restoration work.

TRACI BRIMHALL is the author of *Our Lady of the Ruins* (W. W. Norton, 2012). She teaches at Kansas State University and lives in Manhattan, Kansas.

SALLY ASHTON is the author of *Some Odd Afternoon*, *Her Name Is Juanita*, and *These Metallic Days*. She is Editor-in-Chief of *DMQ Review*, an online journal featuring poetry and art. She was awarded first prize in the Fish Publishing Flash Fiction contest and has work forthcoming in *Brevity*, *Zyzzyva*, and *Poet Lore*. She teaches at San Jose State University.

LISKA JACOBS has been nominated for the Kirkwood Literary Prize in Fiction twice, selected for the New Short Fiction series, and is a recipient of a Squaw Valley Community of Writers' scholarship. She is one of the founding editors of *DUM DUM Zine*, an alt lit publication based in Los Angeles, and is currently pursuing an MFA through the University of California, Riverside. Find more of her work at liskab.tumblr.com.

DIANE SEUSS's most recent collection, *Four-Legged Girl*, was published in 2015 by Graywolf Press. Her second book, *Wolf Lake, White Gown Blown Open*, won the Juniper Prize and was published by the University of Massachusetts Press in 2010. Seuss is Writer in Residence at Kalamazoo College.

KIM YOUNG is the author of *Night Radio*, winner of the 2011 Agha Shahid Ali Poetry Prize (University of Utah Press) and finalist for the 2014 Kate Tufts Discovery Award. She is the founding editor of *Chaparral* — an online journal featuring poetry from Southern California. She teaches at California State University Northridge and lives in LA with her husband and daughter.

PAUL MANDELBAUM is the author of two volumes of linked stories, *Garrett in Wedlock* and *Adriane on the Edge*, and the editor of two literary anthologies, most recently *12 Short Stories and Their Making*. Part of Emerson College's Los Angeles faculty, he also teaches short story writing in the UCLA Extension Writers' Program.

MORGAN PARKER is the author of *Other People's Comfort Keeps Me Up at Night* (Switchback Books, 2015), selected by Eileen Myles for the 2013 Gatewood Prize. Her work has been featured or is forthcoming in numerous publications, as well as anthologized in *Why I Am Not a Painter* (Argos Books) and *The BreakBeat Poets: New American Poetry in the Age of Hip-Hop* (Haymarket Books). She has done editorial work for *Apogee Journal*, *No, Dear Magazine*, and *The Atlas Review*. Winner of a 2016 Pushcart Prize and a Cave Canem graduate fellow, Parker lives with her dog Braeburn in Brooklyn, New York. She works as an editor for Amazon Publishing's imprint Little A, and moonlights as poetry editor of *The Offing*. She also teaches creative writing at Columbia University and co-curates the Poets With Attitude (PWA) reading series with Tommy Pico.

INGRID ROJAS CONTRERAS is the 2014 recipient of the Mary Tanenbaum Award for Nonfiction. Her writing is forthcoming or has been anthologized in *Guernica Annual*, *Wise Latinas* (University of Nebraska Press), and *American Odysseys: Writings by New Americans* (Dalkey Archive Press). She has received fellowships from the San Francisco Writer's Grotto, Bread Loaf, and is the current Community Radio Storytelling Fellow at *Making Contact*, a national radio program. Currently, she is working on a memoir about her grandfather, a medicine man from Colombia who it was said could move clouds.

SVEN BIRKERTS is the editor of the journal *AGNI*. His book *The Other Walk* was published by Graywolf Press in September 2011. His book *Changing the Subject: Art and Attention in the Internet Age* will be published later this year.

SIMONE FORTI
LARGO ARGENTINA (AKA ROME CATS), 1968/2012
C-PRINT, 14 X 20 1/2"
COURTESY OF THE ARTIST AND THE BOX, LA